THE ATHENIAN CONSTITUTION

ARISTOTLE

Published by True Sign Publishing House
Address: SY. No. 21/2 & 21/3, Sonnenahalli,
Krishnarajapural, Bengaluru,
Karnataka - 560049 India
E-mail: truesignbooks@gmail.com
Website: www.truesign.in

The Athenian Constitution
Author: Aristotle

ISBN: 978-93-5462-254-0

First Edition: 2021

Contents

PART-1

...[THEY were tried] by a court empanelled from among the noble families, and sworn upon the sacrifices. The part of accuser was taken by Myron. They were found guilty of the sacrilege, and their bodies were cast out of their graves and their race banished for evermore. In view of this expiation, Epimenides the Cretan performed a purification of the city.

PART-2

AFTER this event there was contention for a long time between the upper classes and the populace. Not only was the constitution at this time oligarchical in every respect, but the poorer classes, men, women, and children, were the serfs of the rich. They were known as Pelatae and also as Hectemori, because they cultivated the lands of the rich at the rent thus indicated. The whole country was in the hands of a few persons, and if the tenants failed to pay their rent they were liable to be haled into slavery, and their children with them. All loans secured upon the debtor's person, a custom which prevailed until the time of Solon, who was the first to appear as the champion of the people. But the hardest and bitterest part of the constitution in the eyes of the masses was their state of serfdom. Not but what they were also discontented with every other feature of their lot; for, to speak generally, they had no part nor share in anything.

PART-3

NOW the ancient constitution, as it existed before the time of Draco, was organized as follows. The magistrates were elected according to qualifications of birth and wealth. At first they governed for life, but subsequently for terms of ten years. The first magistrates, both in date and in importance, were the King, the Polemarch, and the Archon. The earliest of these offices was that of the King, which existed from ancestral antiquity. To this was added, secondly, the office of Polemarch, on account of some of the kings proving feeble in war; for it was on this account that Ion was invited to accept the post on an occasion of pressing need. The last of the three offices was that of the Archon, which most authorities state to have come into existence in the time of Medon. Others assign it to the time of Acastus, and adduce as proof the fact that the nine Archons swear to execute their oaths 'as in the days of Acastus,' which seems to suggest that it was in his time that the descendants of Codrus retired from the kingship in return for the prerogatives conferred upon the Archon. Whichever way it may be, the difference in date is small; but that it was the last of these magistracies to be created is shown by the fact that the Archon has no part in the ancestral sacrifices, as the King and the Polemarch have, but exclusively in those of later origin. So it is only at a comparatively late date that the office of Archon has become of great importance, through the dignity conferred by these later additions. The Thesmothetae were many years afterwards, when these offices had already become annual, with the object that they might publicly record all legal decisions, and act as guardians of them with a view to determining the issues between litigants. Accordingly their office, alone of those which have been mentioned, was never of more than annual duration.

Such, then, is the relative chronological precedence of these offices. At that time the nine Archons did not all live together. The King occupied the building now known as the Boculium, near the Prytaneum, as may be seen from the fact that even to the present day the marriage of the King's wife to Dionysus takes place there. The Archon lived in the Prytaneum, the Polemarch in the Epilyceum. The latter building was formerly called the Polemarcheum, but after Epilycus, during his term of office as Polemarch, had rebuilt it and fitted it up, it was called the Epilyceum. The Thesmothetae occupied the Thesmotheteum. In the time of Solon, however, they all came together into the Thesmotheteum. They had power to decide cases finally on their own authority, not, as now, merely to hold a preliminary hearing. Such then was the arrangement of the magistracies. The Council of Areopagus had as its constitutionally assigned duty the protection of the laws; but in point of fact it administered the greater and most important part of the government of the state, and inflicted personal punishments and fines summarily upon all who misbehaved themselves. This was the natural consequence of the facts that the Archons were elected under qualifications of birth and wealth, and that the Areopagus was composed of those who had served as Archons; for which latter reason the membership of the Areopagus is the only office which has continued to be a life-magistracy to the present day.

PART-4

SUCH was, in outline, the first constitution, but not very long after the events above recorded, in the archonship of Aristaichmus, Draco enacted his ordinances. Now his constitution had the following form. The franchise was given to all who could furnish themselves with a military equipment. The nine Archons and the Treasurers were elected by this body from persons possessing an unencumbered property of not less than ten minas, the less important officials from those who could furnish themselves with a military equipment, and the generals [Strategi] and commanders of the cavalry [Hipparchi] from those who could show an unencumbered property of not less than a hundred minas, and had children born in lawful wedlock over ten years of age. These officers were required to hold to bail the Prytanes, the Strategi, and the Hipparchi of the preceding year until their accounts had been audited, taking four securities of the same class as that to which the Strategi and the Hipparchi belonged. There was also to be a Council, consisting of four hundred and one members, elected by lot from among those who possessed the franchise. Both for this and for the other magistracies the lot was cast among those who were over thirty years of age; and no one might hold office twice until every one else had had his turn, after which they were to cast the lot afresh. If any member of the Council failed to attend when there was a sitting of the Council or of the Assembly, he paid a fine, to the amount of three drachmas if he was a Pentacosiomedimnus, two if he was a Knight, and One if he was a Zeugites. The Council of Areopagus was guardian of the laws, and kept watch over the magistrates to see that they executed their offices in accordance with the laws. Any person who felt himself wronged might lay an information before the Council of Areopagus, on declaring what law was broken by the wrong done to him. But, as has been said before, loans were secured upon the persons of the debtors, and the land was in the hands of a few.

PART-5

SINCE such, then, was the organization of the constitution, and the many were in slavery to the few, the people rose against the upper class. The strife was keen, and for a long time the two parties were ranged in hostile camps against one another, till at last, by common consent, they appointed Solon to be mediator and Archon, and committed the whole constitution to his hands. The immediate occasion of his appointment was his poem, which begins with the words:

I behold, and within my heart deep sadness has claimed its place,
As I mark the oldest home of the ancient Ionian race
Slain by the sword.

In this poem he fights and disputes on behalf of each party in turn against the other, and finally he advises them to come to terms and put an end to the quarrel existing between them. By birth and reputation Solon was one of the foremost men of the day, but in wealth and position he was of the middle class, as is generally agreed, and is, indeed, established by his own evidence in these poems, where he exhorts the wealthy not to be grasping.

But ye who have store of good, who are sated and overflow,
Restrain your swelling soul, and still it and keep it low:
Let the heart that is great within you be trained a lowlier way;
Ye shall not have all at your will, and we will not for ever obey.

Indeed, he constantly fastens the blame of the conflict on the rich; and accordingly at the beginning of the poem he says that he fears 'the love of wealth and an overweening mind', evidently meaning that it was through these that the quarrel arose.

PART-6

As soon as he was at the head of affairs, Solon liberated the people once and for all, by prohibiting all loans on the security of the debtor's person: and in addition he made laws by which he cancelled all debts, public and private. This measure is commonly called the Seisachtheia [= removal of burdens], since thereby the people had their loads removed from them. In connexion with it some persons try to traduce the character of Solon. It so happened that, when he was about to enact the Seisachtheia, he communicated his intention to some members of the upper class, whereupon, as the partisans of the popular party say, his friends stole a march on him; while those who wish to attack his character maintain that he too had a share in the fraud himself. For these persons borrowed money and bought up a large amount of land, and so when, a short time afterwards, all debts were cancelled, they became wealthy; and this, they say, was the origin of the families which were afterwards looked on as having been wealthy from primeval times. However, the story of the popular party is by far the most probable. A man who was so moderate and public-spirited in all his other actions, that when it was within his power to put his fellow-citizens beneath his feet and establish himself as tyrant, he preferred instead to incur the hostility of both parties by placing his honour and the general welfare above his personal aggrandisement, is not likely to have consented to defile his hands by such a petty and palpable fraud. That he had this absolute power is, in the first place, indicated by the desperate condition the country; moreover, he mentions it himself repeatedly in his poems, and it is universally admitted. We are therefore bound to consider this accusation to be false.

PART-7

NEXT Solon drew up a constitution and enacted new laws; and the ordinances of Draco ceased to be used, with the exception of those relating to murder. The laws were inscribed on the wooden stands, and set up in the King's Porch, and all swore to obey them; and the nine Archons made oath upon the stone, declaring that they would dedicate a golden statue if they should transgress any of them. This is the origin of the oath to that effect which they take to the present day. Solon ratified his laws for a hundred years; and the following was the fashion in which he organized the constitution. He divided the population according to property into four classes, just as it had been divided before, namely, Pentacosiomedimni, Knights, Zeugitae, and Thetes. The various magistracies, namely, the nine Archons, the Treasurers, the Commissioners for Public Contracts (Poletae), the Eleven, and Clerks (Colacretae), he assigned to the Pentacosiomedimni, the Knights, and the Zeugitae, giving offices to each class in proportion to the value of their rateable property. To who ranked among the Thetes he gave nothing but a place in the Assembly and in the juries. A man had to rank as a Pentacosiomedimnus if he made, from his own land, five hundred measures, whether liquid or solid. Those ranked as Knights who made three hundred measures, or, as some say, those who were able to maintain a horse. In support of the latter definition they adduce the name of the class, which may be supposed to be derived from this fact, and also some votive offerings of early times; for in the

Acropolis there is a votive offering, a statue of Diphilus, bearing this inscription:

> The son of Diphilus, Athenion hight,
> Raised from the Thetes and become a knight,
> Did to the gods this sculptured charger bring,
> For his promotion a thank-offering.

And a horse stands in evidence beside the man, implying that this was what was meant by belonging to the rank of Knight. At the same time it seems reasonable to suppose that this class, like the Pentacosiomedimni, was defined by the possession of an income of a certain number of measures. Those ranked as Zeugitae who made two hundred measures, liquid or solid; and the rest ranked as Thetes, and were not eligible for any office. Hence it is that even at the present day, when a candidate for any office is asked to what class he belongs, no one would think of saying that he belonged to the Thetes.

PART-8

THE elections to the various offices Solon enacted should be by lot, out of candidates selected by each of the tribes. Each tribe selected ten candidates for the nine archonships, and among these the lot was cast. Hence it is still the custom for each tribe to choose ten candidates by lot, and then the lot is again cast among these. A proof that Solon regulated the elections to office according to the property classes may be found in the law still in force with regard to the Treasurers, which enacts that they shall be chosen from the Pentacosiomedimni. Such was Solon's legislation with respect to the nine Archons; whereas in early times the Council of Areopagus summoned suitable persons according to its own judgement and appointed them for the year to the several offices. There were four tribes, as before, and four tribe-kings. Each tribe was divided into three Trittyes [=Thirds], with twelve Naucraries in each; and the Naucraries had officers of their own, called Naucrari, whose duty it was to superintend the current receipts and expenditure. Hence, among the laws of Solon now obsolete, it is repeatedly written that the Naucrari are to receive and to spend out of the Naucraric fund. Solon also appointed a Council of four hundred, a hundred from each tribe; but he assigned to the Council of the Areopagus the duty of superintending the laws, acting as before as the guardian of the constitution in general. It kept watch over the affairs of the state in most of the more important matters, and corrected offenders, with full powers to inflict either fines or personal punishment. The money received in fines it brought up into the Acropolis, without assigning the reason for the mulct. It also tried those who conspired for the overthrow of the state, Solon having enacted a process of impeachment to deal with such offenders. Further, since he saw the state often engaged in internal disputes, while many of the citizens from sheer indifference accepted whatever might turn up, he made a law with express reference to such persons, enacting that any one who, in a time [Transcriber's note: of?] civil factions, did not take up arms with either party, should lose his rights as a citizen and cease to have any part in the state.

PART-9

SUCH, then, was his legislation concerning the magistracies. There are three points in the constitution of Solon which appear to be its most democratic features: first and most important, the prohibition of loans on the security of the debtor's person; secondly, the right of every person who so willed to claim redress on behalf of any one to whom wrong was being done; thirdly, the institution of the appeal to the jurycourts; and it is to this last, they say, that the masses have owed their strength most of all, since, when the democracy is master of the voting-power, it is master of the constitution. Moreover, since the laws were not drawn up in simple and explicit terms (but like the one concerning inheritances and wards of state), disputes inevitably occurred, and the courts had to decide in every matter, whether public or private. Some persons in fact believe that Solon deliberately made the laws indefinite, in order that the final decision might be in the hands of the people. This, however, is not probable, and the reason no doubt was that it is impossible to attain ideal perfection when framing a law in general terms; for we must judge of his intentions, not from the actual results in the present day, but from the general tenor of the rest of his legislation.

PART-10

THESE seem to be the democratic features of his laws; but in addition, before the period of his legislation, he carried through his abolition of debts, and after it his increase in the standards of weights and measures, and of the currency. During his administration the measures were made larger than those of Pheidon, and the mina, which previously had a standard of seventy drachmas, was raised to the full hundred. The standard coin in earlier times was the two-drachma piece. He also made weights corresponding with the coinage, sixty-three minas going to the talent; and the odd three minas were distributed among the staters and the other values.

PART-11

WHEN he had completed his organization of the constitution in the manner that has been described, he found himself beset by people coming to him and harassing him concerning his laws, criticizing here and questioning there, till, as he wished neither to alter what he had decided on nor yet to be an object of ill will to every one by remaining in Athens, he set off on a journey to Egypt, with the combined objects of trade and travel, giving out that he should not return for ten years. He considered that there was no call for him to expound the laws personally, but that every one should obey them just as they were written. Moreover, his position at this time was unpleasant. Many members of the upper class had been estranged from him on account of his abolition of debts, and both parties were alienated through their disappointment at the condition of things which he had created. The mass of the people had expected him to make a complete redistribution of all property, and the upper class hoped he would restore everything to its former position, or, at any rate, make but a small change. Solon, however, had resisted both classes. He might have made himself a despot by attaching himself to whichever party he chose, but he preferred, though at the cost of incurring the enmity of both, to be the saviour of his country and the ideal lawgiver.

PART-12

THE truth of this view of Solon's policy is established alike by common consent, and by the mention he has himself made of the matter in his poems. Thus:

> I gave to the mass of the people such rank as befitted their need,
> I took not away their honour, and I granted naught to their greed;

While those who were rich in power, who in wealth were glorious and great,
I bethought me that naught should befall them unworthy their splendour and state;
So I stood with my shield outstretched, and both were safe in its sight,
And I would not that either should triumph, when the triumph was not with right.

Again he declares how the mass of the people ought to be treated:

But thus will the people best the voice of their leaders obey,
When neither too slack is the rein, nor violence holdeth the sway;
For indulgence breedeth a child, the presumption that spurns control,
When riches too great are poured upon men of unbalanced soul.

And again elsewhere he speaks about the persons who wished to redistribute the land:

So they came in search of plunder, and their cravings knew no bound,
Every one among them deeming endless wealth would here be found.
And that I with glozing smoothness hid a cruel mind within.
Fondly then and vainly dreamt they; now they raise an angry din,
And they glare askance in anger, and the light within their eyes
Burns with hostile flames upon me. Yet therein no justice lies.
All I promised, fully wrought I with the gods at hand to cheer,
Naught beyond in folly ventured. Never to my soul was dear
With a tyrant's force to govern, nor to see the good and base
Side by side in equal portion share the rich home of our race.

Once more he speaks of the abolition of debts and of those who before were in servitude, but were released owing to the Seisachtheia:

Of all the aims for which I summoned forth
The people, was there one I compassed not?
Thou, when slow time brings justice in its train,
O mighty mother of the Olympian gods,
Dark Earth, thou best canst witness, from whose breast
I swept the pillars broadcast planted there,
And made thee free, who hadst been slave of yore.
And many a man whom fraud or law had sold
For from his god-built land, an outcast slave,
I brought again to Athens; yea, and some,

Exiles from home through debt's oppressive load,
Speaking no more the dear ATHENIAN tongue,
But wandering far and wide, I brought again;

And those that here in vilest slavery
Crouched 'neath a master's frown, I set them free.
Thus might and right were yoked in harmony,
Since by the force of law I won my ends
And kept my promise. Equal laws I gave
To evil and to good, with even hand
Drawing straight justice for the lot of each.
But had another held the goad as
One in whose heart was guile and greediness,
He had not kept the people back from strife.
For had I granted, now what pleased the one,
Then what their foes devised in counterpoise,
Of many a man this state had been bereft.
Therefore I showed my might on every side,
Turning at bay like wolf among the hounds.

And again he reviles both parties for their grumblings in the times that followed:

Nay, if one must lay blame where blame is due,
Wer't not for me, the people ne'er had set
Their eyes upon these blessings e'en in dreams:
While greater men, the men of wealthier life,
Should praise me and should court me as their friend.

For had any other man, he says, received this exalted post,

He had not kept the people back, nor ceased
Til he had robbed the richness of the milk.
But I stood forth a landmark in the midst,
And barred the foes from battle.

PART-13

SUCH then, were Solon's reasons for his departure from the country. After his retirement the city was still torn by divisions. For four years, indeed, they lived in peace; but in the fifth year after Solon's government they were unable to elect an Archon on account of their dissensions, and again four years later they elected no Archon for the same reason. Subsequently, after a similar period had elapsed, Damasias was elected Archon; and he governed for two years and two months, until he was forcibly expelled from his office. After this, it was agreed, as a compromise, to elect ten Archons, five from the Eupatridae, three from the Agroeci, and two from the Demiurgi, and they ruled for the year following Damasias. It is clear from this that the Archon was at the time the magistrate who possessed the greatest power, since it is always in connexion with this office that conflicts are seen to arise. But altogether they were in a continual state of internal disorder. Some found the cause and justification of their discontent in the abolition of debts, because thereby they had been reduced to poverty; others were dissatisfied with the political constitution, because it had undergone a revolutionary change; while with others the motive was found in personal rivalries among themselves. The parties at this time were three in number. First there was the party of the Shore, led by Megacles the son of Alcmeon, which was considered to aim at a moderate form of government; then there were the men of the Plain, who desired an oligarchy and were led by Lycurgus; and thirdly there were the men of the Highlands, at the head of whom was Pisistratus, who was looked on as an extreme democrat. This latter party was reinforced by those who had been deprived of the debts due to them, from motives of poverty, and by those who were not of pure descent, from motives of personal apprehension. A proof of this is seen in the fact that after the tyranny was overthrown a revision was made of the citizen-roll, on the ground that many persons were partaking in the franchise without having a right to it. The names given to the respective parties were derived from the districts in which they held their lands.

PART-14

PISISTRATUS had the reputation of being an extreme democrat, and he also had distinguished himself greatly in the war with Megara. Taking advantage of this, he wounded himself, and by representing that his injuries had been inflicted on him by his political rivals, he persuaded the people, through a motion proposed by Aristion, to grant him a bodyguard. After he had got these 'club-bearers', as they were called, he made an attack with them on the people and seized the Acropolis. This happened in the archonship of Comeas, thirty-one years after the legislation of Solon. It is related that, when Pisistratus asked for his bodyguard, Solon opposed the request, and declared that in so doing he proved himself wiser than half the people and braver than the rest,--wiser than those who did not see that Pisistratus designed to make himself tyrant, and braver than those who saw it and kept silence. But when all his words availed nothing he carried forth his armour and set it up in front of his house, saying that he had helped his country so far as lay in his power (he was already a very old man), and that he called on all others to do the same. Solon's exhortations, however, proved fruitless, and Pisistratus assumed the sovereignty. His administration was more like a constitutional government than the rule of a tyrant; but before his power was firmly established, the adherents of Megacles and Lycurgus made a coalition and drove him out. This took place in the archonship of Hegesias, five years after the first establishment of his rule. Eleven years later Megacles, being in difficulties in a party struggle, again opened negotiations with Pisistratus, proposing that the latter should marry his daughter; and on these terms he brought him back to Athens, by a very primitive and simple-minded device. He first spread abroad a rumour that Athens was bringing back Pisistratus, and then, having found a woman of great stature and beauty, named Phye (according to Herodotus, of the deme of Paeania, but as others say a Thracian flower-seller of the deme of Collytus), he dressed her in a garb resembling that of the goddess and brought her into the city with Pisistratus. The latter drove in on a chariot with the woman beside him, and the inhabitants of the city, struck with awe, received him with adoration.

PART-15

In this manner did his first return take place. He did not, however, hold his power long, for about six years after his return he was again expelled. He refused to treat the daughter of Megacles as his wife, and being afraid, in consequence, of a combination of the two opposing parties, he retired from the country. First he led a colony to a place called Rhaicelus, in the region of the Thermaic gulf; and thence he passed to the country in the neighbourhood of Mt. Pangaeus. Here he acquired wealth and hired mercenaries; and not till ten years had elapsed did he return to Eretria and make an attempt to recover the government by force. In this he had the assistance of many allies, notably the Thebans and Lygdamis of Naxos, and also the Knights who held the supreme power in the constitution of Eretria. After his victory in the battle at Pallene he captured Athens, and when he had disarmed the people he at last had his tyranny securely established, and was able to take Naxos and set up Lygdamis as ruler there. He effected the disarmament of the people in the following manner. He ordered a parade in full armour in the Theseum, and began to make a speech to the people. He spoke for a short time, until the people called out that they could not hear him, whereupon he bade them come up to the entrance of the Acropolis, in order that his voice might be better heard. Then, while he continued to speak to them at great length, men whom he had appointed for the purpose collected the arms and locked them up in the chambers of the Theseum hard by, and came and made a signal to him that it was done. Pisistratus accordingly, when he had finished the rest of what he had to say, told the people also what had happened to their arms; adding that they were not to be surprised or alarmed, but go home and attend to their private affairs, while he would himself for the future manage all the business of the state.

PART-16

SUCH was the origin and such the vicissitudes of the tyranny of Pisistratus. His administration was temperate, as has been said before, and more like constitutional government than a tyranny. Not only was he in every respect humane and mild and ready to forgive those who offended, but, in addition, he advanced money to the poorer people to help them in their labours, so that they might make their living by agriculture. In this he had two objects, first that they might not spend their time in the city but might be scattered over all the face of the country, and secondly that, being moderately well off and occupied with their own business, they might have neither the wish nor the time to attend to public affairs. At the same time his revenues were increased by the thorough cultivation of the country, since he imposed a tax of one tenth on all the produce. For the same reasons he instituted the local justices, and often made expeditions in person into the country to inspect it and to settle disputes between individuals, that they might not come into the city and neglect their farms. It was in one of these progresses that, as the story goes, Pisistratus had his adventure with the man of Hymettus, who was cultivating the spot afterwards known as 'Tax-free Farm'. He saw a man digging and working at a very stony piece of ground, and being surprised he sent his attendant to ask what he got out of this plot of land. 'Aches and pains', said the man; 'and that's what Pisistratus ought to have his tenth of'. The man spoke without knowing who his questioner was; but Pisistratus was so pleased with his frank speech and his industry that he granted him exemption from all taxes. And so in matters in general he burdened the people as little as possible with his government, but always cultivated peace and kept them in all quietness. Hence the tyranny of Pisistratus was often spoken of proverbially as 'the age of gold'; for when his sons succeeded him the government became much harsher. But most important of all in this respect was his popular and kindly disposition. In all things he was accustomed to observe the laws, without giving himself any exceptional privileges. Once he was summoned on a charge of homicide before the Areopagus, and he appeared in person to make his defence; but the prosecutor was afraid to present himself and abandoned the case. For these reasons he held power long, and whenever he was expelled he regained his position easily. The majority alike of the upper class and of the people were in his favour; the former he won by his social intercourse with them, the latter by the assistance which he gave to their private purses, and his nature fitted him to win the hearts of both. Moreover, the laws in reference to tyrants at that time in force at Athens were very mild, especially the one which applies more particularly to the establishment of a tyranny. The law ran as follows: 'These are the ancestral statutes of the ATHENIANs; if any persons shall make an attempt to establish a tyranny, or if any person shall join in setting up a tyranny, he shall lose his civic rights, both himself and his whole house.'

PART-17

THUS did Pisistratus grow old in the possession of power, and he died a natural death in the archonship of Philoneos, three and thirty years from the time at which he first established himself as tyrant, during nineteen of which he was in possession of power; the rest he spent in exile. It is evident from this that the story is mere gossip which states that Pisistratus was the youthful favourite of Solon and commanded in the war against Megara for the recovery of Salamis. It will not harmonize with their respective ages, as any one may see who will reckon up the years of the life of each of them, and the dates at which they died. After the death of Pisistratus his sons took up the government, and conducted it on the same system. He had two sons by his first and legitimate wife, Hippias and Hipparchus, and two by his Argive consort, Iophon and

Hegesistratus, who was surnamed Thessalus. For Pisistratus took a wife from Argos, Timonassa, the daughter of a man of Argos, named Gorgilus; she had previously been the wife of Archinus of Ambracia, one of the descendants of Cypselus. This was the origin of his friendship with the Argives, on account of which a thousand of them were brought over by Hegesistratus and fought on his side in the battle at Pallene. Some authorities say that this marriage took place after his first expulsion from Athens, others while he was in possession of the government.

PART-18

HIPPIAS and Hipparchus assumed the control of affairs on grounds alike of standing and of age; but Hippias, as being also naturally of a statesmanlike and shrewd disposition, was really the head of the government. Hipparchus was youthful in disposition, amorous, and fond of literature (it was he who invited to Athens Anacreon, Simonides, and the other poets), while Thessalus was much junior in age, and was violent and headstrong in his behaviour. It was from his character that all the evils arose which befell the house. He became enamoured of Harmodius, and, since he failed to win his affection, he lost all restraint upon his passion, and in addition to other exhibitions of rage he finally prevented the sister of Harmodius from taking the part of a basket-bearer in the Panathenaic procession, alleging as his reason that Harmodius was a person of loose life. Thereupon, in a frenzy of wrath, Harmodius and Aristogeiton did their celebrated deed, in conjunction with a number of confederates. But while they were lying in wait for Hippias in the Acropolis at the time of the Panathenaea (Hippias, at this moment, was awaiting the arrival of the procession, while Hipparchus was organizing its dispatch) they saw one of the persons privy to the plot talking familiarly with him. Thinking that he was betraying them, and desiring to do something before they were arrested, they rushed down and made their attempt without waiting for the rest of their confederates. They succeeded in killing Hipparchus near the Leocoreum while he was engaged in arranging the procession, but ruined the design as a whole; of the two leaders, Harmodius was killed on the spot by the guards, while Aristogeiton was arrested, and perished later after suffering long tortures. While under the torture he accused many persons who belonged by birth to the most distinguished families and were also personal friends of the tyrants. At first the government could find no clue to the conspiracy; for the current story, that Hippias made all who were taking part in the procession leave their arms, and then detected those who were carrying secret daggers, cannot be true, since at that time they did not bear arms in the processions, this being a custom instituted at a later period by the democracy. According to the story of the popular party, Aristogeiton accused the friends of the tyrants with the deliberate intention that the latter might commit an impious act, and at the same time weaken themselves, by putting to death innocent men who were their own friends; others say that he told no falsehood, but was betraying the actual accomplices. At last, when for all his efforts he could not obtain release by death, he promised to give further information against a number of other persons; and, having induced Hippias to give him his hand to confirm his word, as soon as he had hold of it he reviled him for giving his hand to the murderer of his brother, till Hippias, in a frenzy of rage, lost control of himself and snatched out his dagger and dispatched him.

PART-19

AFTER this event the tyranny became much harsher. In consequence of his vengeance for his brother, and of the execution and banishment of a large number of persons, Hippias became a distrusted and an embittered man. About three years after the death of Hipparchus, finding his position in the city insecure, he set about fortifying Munichia, with the intention of establishing himself there. While he was still engaged on this work, however, he was expelled by Cleomenes, king of Lacedaemon, in consequence of the Spartans being continually incited by oracles to overthrow the tyranny. These oracles were obtained in the following way. The Athenian exiles, headed by the Alcmeonidae, could not by their own power effect their return, but failed continually in their attempts. Among their other failures, they fortified a post in Attica, Lipsydrium, above Mt. Parnes, and were there joined by some partisans from the city; but they were besieged by the tyrants and reduced to surrender. After this disaster the following became a popular drinking song:

Ah! Lipsydrium, faithless friend!
Lo, what heroes to death didst send,
Nobly born and great in deed!
Well did they prove themselves at need
Of noble sires a noble seed.

Having failed, then, in every other method, they took the contract for rebuilding the temple at Delphi, thereby obtaining ample funds, which they employed to secure the help of the Lacedaemonians. All this time the Pythia kept continually enjoining on the Lacedaemonians who came to consult the oracle, that they must free Athens; till finally she succeeded in impelling the Spartans to that step, although the house of Pisistratus was connected with them by ties of hospitality. The resolution of the Lacedaemonians was, however, at least equally due to the friendship which had been formed between the house of Pisistratus and Argos. Accordingly they first sent Anchimolus by sea at the head of an army; but he was defeated and killed, through the arrival of Cineas of Thessaly to support the sons of Pisistratus with a force of a thousand horsemen. Then, being roused to anger by this disaster, they sent their king, Cleomenes, by land at the head of a larger force; and he, after defeating the Thessalian cavalry when they attempted to intercept his march into Attica, shut up Hippias within what was known as the Pelargic wall and blockaded him there with the assistance of the Athenians. While he was sitting down before the place, it so happened that the sons of the Pisistratidae were captured in an attempt to slip out; upon which the tyrants capitulated on condition of the safety of their children, and surrendered the Acropolis to the Athenians, five days being first allowed them to remove their effects. This took place in the archonship of Harpactides, after they had held the tyranny for about seventeen years since their father's death, or in all, including the period of their father's rule, for nine-and-forty years.

PART-20

AFTER the overthrow of the tyranny, the rival leaders in the state were Isagoras son of Tisander, a partisan of the tyrants, and Cleisthenes, who belonged to the family of the Alcmeonidae. Cleisthenes, being beaten in the political clubs, called in the people by giving the franchise to the masses. Thereupon Isagoras, finding himself left inferior in power, invited Cleomenes, who was united to him by ties of hospitality, to return to Athens, and persuaded him to 'drive out the pollution', a plea derived from the fact that the Alcmeonidae were suppposed to be under the curse of pollution. On this Cleisthenes retired from the country, and Cleomenes, entering Attica with a small force, expelled, as polluted, seven hundred Athenian families. Having effected this, he next attempted to dissolve the Council, and to set up Isagoras and three hundred of his partisans as the supreme power in the state. The Council, however, resisted, the populace flocked together, and Cleomenes and Isagoras, with their adherents, took refuge in the Acropolis. Here the people sat down and besieged them for two days; and on the third they agreed to let Cleomenes and all his followers depart, while they summoned Cleisthenes and the other exiles back to Athens. When the people had thus obtained the command of affairs, Cleisthenes was their chief and popular leader. And this was natural; for the Alcmeonidae were perhaps the chief cause of the expulsion of the tyrants, and for the greater part of their rule were at perpetual war with them. But even earlier than the attempts of the Alcmeonidae, one Cedon made an attack on the tyrants; when there came another popular drinking song, addressed to him:

Pour a health yet again, boy, to Cedon; forget not this duty to do,
If a health is an honour befitting the name of a good man and true.

PART-21

THE people, therefore, had good reason to place confidence in Cleisthenes. Accordingly, now that he was the popular leader, three years after the expulsion of the tyrants, in the archonship of Isagoras, his first step was to distribute the whole population into ten tribes in place of the existing four, with the object of intermixing the members of the different tribes, and so securing that more persons might have a share in the franchise. From this arose the saying 'Do not look at the tribes', addressed to those who wished to scrutinize the lists of the old families. Next he made the Council to consist of five hundred members instead of four hundred, each tribe now contributing fifty, whereas formerly each had sent a hundred. The reason why he did not organize the people into twelve tribes was that he might not have to use the existing division into trittyes; for the four tribes had twelve trittyes, so that he would not have achieved his object of redistributing the population in fresh combinations. Further, he divided the country into thirty groups of demes, ten from the districts about the city, ten from the coast, and ten from the interior. These he called trittyes; and he assigned three of them by lot to each tribe, in such a way that each should have one portion in each of these three localities. All who lived in any given deme he declared fellow-demesmen, to the end that the new citizens might not be exposed by the habitual use of family names, but that men might be officially described by the names of their demes; and accordingly it is by the names of their demes that the

Athenians speak of one another. He also instituted Demarchs, who had the same duties as the previously existing Naucrari,--the demes being made to take the place of the naucraries. He gave names to the demes, some from the localities to which they belonged, some from the persons who founded them, since some of the areas no longer corresponded to localities possessing names. On the other hand he allowed every one to retain his family and clan and religious rites according to ancestral custom. The names given to the tribes were the ten which the Pythia appointed out of the hundred selected national heroes.

PART-22

By these reforms the constitution became much more democratic than that of Solon. The laws of Solon had been obliterated by disuse during the period of the tyranny, while Cleisthenes substituted new ones with the object of securing the goodwill of the masses. Among these was the law concerning ostracism. Four years after the establishment of this system, in the archonship of Hermocreon, they first imposed upon the Council of Five Hundred the oath which they take to the present day. Next they began to elect the generals by tribes, one from each tribe, while the Polemarch was the commander of the whole army. Then, eleven years later, in the archonship of Phaenippus they won the battle of Marathon; and two years after this victory, when the people had now gained self-confidence, they for the first time made use of the law of ostracism. This had originally been passed as a precaution against men in high office, because Pisistratus took advantage of his position as a popular leader and general to make himself tyrant; and the first person ostracized was one of his relatives, Hipparchus son of Charmus, of the deme of Collytus, the very person on whose account especially Cleisthenes had enacted the law, as he wished to get rid of him. Hitherto, however, he had escaped; for the Athenians, with the usual leniency of the democracy, allowed all the partisans of the tyrants, who had not joined in their evil deeds in the time of the troubles to remain in the city; and the chief and leader of these was Hipparchus. Then in the very next year, in the archonship of Telesinus, they for the first time since the tyranny elected, tribe by tribe, the nine Archons by lot out of the five hundred candidates selected by the demes, all the earlier ones having been elected by vote; and in the same year Megacles son of Hippocrates, of the deme of Alopece, was ostracized. Thus for three years they continued to ostracize the friends of the tyrants, on whose account the law had been passed; but in the following year they began to remove others as well, including any one who seemed to be more powerful than was expedient. The first person unconnected with the tyrants who was ostracized was Xanthippus son of Ariphron. Two years later, in the archonship of Nicodemus, the mines of Maroneia were discovered, and the state made a profit of a hundred talents from the working of them. Some persons advised the people to make a distribution of the money among themselves, but this was prevented by Themistocles. He refused to say on what he proposed to spend the money, but he bade them lend it to the hundred richest men in Athens, one talent to each, and then, if the manner in which it was employed pleased the people, the expenditure should be charged to the state, but otherwise the state should receive the sum back from those to whom it was lent. On these terms he received the money and with it he had a hundred triremes built, each of the hundred individuals building one; and it was with these ships that they fought the battle of Salamis against the barbarians. About this time Aristides the son of Lysimachus was ostracized. Three years later, however, in the archonship of Hypsichides, all the ostracized persons were recalled, on account of the advance of the army of Xerxes; and it was laid down for the future that persons under sentence of ostracism must live between Geraestus and Scyllaeum, on pain of losing their civic rights irrevocably.

PART-23

So far, then, had the city progressed by this time, growing gradually with the growth of the democracy; but after the Persian wars the Council of Areopagus once more developed strength and assumed the control of the state. It did not acquire this supremacy by virtue of any formal decree, but because it had been the cause of the battle of Salamis being fought. When the generals were utterly at a loss how to meet the crisis and made proclamation that every one should see to his own safety, the Areopagus provided a donation of money, distributing eight drachmas to each member of the ships' crews, and so prevailed on them to go on board. On these grounds people bowed to its prestige; and during this period Athens was well administered. At this time they devoted themselves to the prosecution of the war and were in high repute among the Greeks, so that the command by sea was conferred upon them, in spite of the opposition of the Lacedaemonians. The leaders of the people during this period were Aristides, of Lysimachus, and Themistocles, son of Lysimachus, and Themistocles, son of Neocles, of whom the latter appeared to devote himself to the conduct of war, while the former had the reputation of being a clever statesman and the most upright man of his time. Accordingly the one was usually employed as general, the other as political adviser. The rebuilding of the fortifications they conducted in combination, although they were political opponents; but it was Aristides who, seizing the opportunity afforded by the discredit brought upon the Lacedaemonians by Pausanias, guided the public policy in the matter of the defection of the Ionian states from the alliance with Sparta. It follows that it was he who made the first assessment of tribute from the various allied states, two years after the battle of Salamis, in the archonship of Timosthenes; and it was he who took the oath of offensive and defensive alliance with the Ionians, on which occasion they cast the masses of iron into the sea.

PART-24

AFTER this, seeing the state growing in confidence and much wealth accumulated, he advised the people to lay hold of the leadership of the league, and to quit the country districts and settle in the city. He pointed out to them that all would be able to gain a living there, some by service in the army, others in the garrisons, others by taking a part in public affairs; and in this way they would secure the leadership. This advice was taken; and when the people had assumed the supreme control they proceeded to treat their allies in a more imperious fashion, with the exception of the Chians, Lesbians, and Samians. These they maintained to protect their empire, leaving their constitutions untouched, and allowing them to retain whatever dominion they then possessed. They also secured an ample maintenance for the mass of the population in the way which Aristides had pointed out to them. Out of the proceeds of the tributes and the taxes and the contributions of the allies more than twenty thousand persons were maintained. There were 6,000 jurymen, 1,600 bowmen, 1,200 Knights, 500 members of the Council, 500 guards of the dockyards, besides fifty guards in the Acropolis. There were some 700 magistrates at home, and some 700 abroad. Further, when they subsequently went to war, there were in addition 2,500 heavy-armed troops, twenty guard-ships, and other ships which collected the tributes, with crews amounting to 2,000 men, selected by lot; and besides these there were the persons maintained at the Prytaneum, and orphans, and gaolers, since all these were supported by the state.

PART-25

SUCH was the way in which the people earned their livelihood. The supremacy of the Areopagus lasted for about seventeen years after the Persian wars, although gradually declining. But as the strength of the masses increased, Ephialtes, son of Sophonides, a man with a reputation for incorruptibility and public virtue, who had become the leader of the people, made an attack upon that Council. First of all he ruined many of its members by bringing actions against them with reference to their administration. Then, in the archonship of Conon, he stripped the Council of all the acquired prerogatives from which it derived its guardianship of the constitution, and assigned some of them to the Council of Five Hundred, and others to the Assembly and the law-courts. In this revolution he was assisted by Themistocles, who was himself a member of the Areopagus, but was expecting to be tried before it on a charge of treasonable dealings with Persia. This made him anxious that it should be overthrown, and accordingly he warned Ephialtes that the Council intended to arrest him, while at the same time he informed the Areopagites that he would reveal to them certain persons who were conspiring to subvert the constitution. He then conducted the representatives delegated by the Council to the residence of Ephialtes, promising to show them the conspirators who assembled there, and proceeded to converse with them in an earnest manner. Ephialtes, seeing this, was seized with alarm and took refuge in suppliant guise at the altar. Every one was astounded at the occurrence, and presently, when the Council of Five Hundred met, Ephialtes and Themistocles together proceeded to denounce the Areopagus to them. This they repeated in similar fashion in the Assembly, until they succeeded in depriving it of its power. Not long afterwards, however, Ephialtes was assassinated by Aristodicus of Tanagra. In this way was the Council of Areopagus deprived of its guardianship of the state.

PART-26

AFTER this revolution the administration of the state became more and more lax, in consequence of the eager rivalry of candidates for popular favour. During this period the moderate party, as it happened, had no real chief; their leader being Cimon son of Miltiades, who was a comparatively young man, and had been late in entering public life; and at the same time the general populace suffered great losses by war. The soldiers for active service were selected at that time from the roll of citizens, and as the generals were men of no military experience, who owed their position solely to their family standing, it continually happened that some two or three thousand of the troops perished on an expedition; and in this way the best men alike of the lower and the upper classes were exhausted. Consequently in most matters of administration less heed was paid to the laws than had formerly been the case. No alteration, however, was made in the method of election of the nine Archons, except that five years after the death of Ephialtes it was decided that the candidates to be submitted to the lot for that office might be selected from the Zeugitae as well as from the higher classes. The first Archon from that class was Mnesitheides. Up to this time all the Archons had been taken from the Pentacosiomedimni and Knights, while the Zeugitae were confined to the ordinary magistracies, save where an evasion of the law was overlooked. Four years later, in the archonship of Lysicrates, thirty 'local justices', as they as they were called, were re-established; and two years afterwards, in the archonship of Antidotus, consequence of the great increase in the number of citizens, it was resolved, on the motion of Pericles, that no one should be admitted to the franchise who was not of citizen birth by both parents.

PART-27

AFTER this Pericles came forward as popular leader, having first distinguished himself while still a young man by prosecuting Cimon on the audit of his official accounts as general. Under his auspices the constitution became still more democratic. He took away some of the privileges of the Areopagus, and, above all, he turned the policy of the state in the direction of sea power, which caused the masses to acquire confidence in themselves and consequently to take the conduct of affairs more and more into their own hands. Moreover, forty-eight years after the battle of Salamis, in the archonship of Pythodorus, the Peloponnesian war broke out, during which the populace was shut up in the city and became accustomed to gain its livelihood by military service, and so, partly voluntarily and partly involuntarily, determined to assume the administration of the state itself. Pericles was also the first to institute pay for service in the law-courts, as a bid for popular favour to counterbalance the wealth of Cimon. The latter, having private possessions on a regal scale, not only performed the regular public services magnificently, but also maintained a large number of his fellow-demesmen. Any member of the deme of Laciadae could go every day to Cimon's house and there receive a reasonable provision; while his estate was guarded by no fences, so that any one who liked might help himself to the fruit from it. Pericles' private property was quite unequal to this magnificence and accordingly he took the advice of Damonides of Oia (who was commonly supposed to be the person who prompted Pericles in most of his measures, and was therefore subsequently ostracized), which was that, as he was beaten in the matter of private possessions, he should make gifts to the people from their own property; and accordingly he instituted pay for the members of the juries. Some critics accuse him of thereby causing a deterioration in the character of the juries, since it was always the common people who put themselves forward for selection as jurors, rather than the men of better position. Moreover, bribery came into existence after this, the first person to introduce it being Anytus, after his command at Pylos. He was prosecuted by certain individuals on account of his loss of Pylos, but escaped by bribing the jury.

PART-28

So long, however, as Pericles was leader of the people, things went tolerably well with the state; but when he was dead there was a great change for the worse. Then for the first time did the people choose a leader who was of no reputation among men of good standing, whereas up to this time such men had always been found as leaders of the democracy. The first leader of the people, in the very beginning of things, was Solon, and the second was Pisistratus, both of them men of birth and position. After the overthrow of the tyrants there was Cleisthenes, a member of the house of the Alcmeonidae; and he had no rival opposed to him after the expulsion of the party of Isagoras. After this Xanthippus was the leader of the people, and Miltiades of the upper class. Then came Themistocles and Aristides, and after them Ephialtes as leader of the people, and Cimon son of Miltiades of the wealthier class. Pericles followed as leader of the people, and Thucydides, who was connected by marriage with Cimon, of the opposition. After the death of Pericles, Nicias, who subsequently fell in Sicily, appeared as leader of the aristocracy, and Cleon son of Cleaenetus of the people. The latter seems, more than any one else, to have been the cause of the corruption of the democracy by his wild undertakings; and he was the first to use unseemly shouting and coarse abuse on the Bema, and to harangue the people with his cloak girt up short about him, whereas all his predecessors had spoken decently and in order. These were succeeded by Theramenes son of Hagnon as leader of the one party, and the lyre-maker Cleophon of the people. It was Cleophon who first granted the two-obol donation for the theatrical performances, and for some time it continued to be given; but then Callicrates of Paeania ousted him by promising to add a third obol to the sum. Both of these persons were subsequently condemned to death; for the people, even if they are deceived for a time, in the end generally come to detest those who have beguiled them into any unworthy action. After Cleophon the popular leadership was occupied successively by the men who chose to talk the biggest and pander the most to the tastes of the majority, with their eyes fixed only on the interests of the moment. The best statesmen at Athens, after those of early times, seem to have been Nicias, Thucydides, and Theramenes. As to Nicias and Thucydides, nearly every one agrees that they were not merely men of birth and character, but also statesmen, and that they ruled the state with paternal care. On the merits of Theramenes opinion is divided, because it so happened that in his time public affairs were in a very stormy state. But those who give their opinion deliberately find him, not, as his critics falsely assert, overthrowing every kind of constitution, but supporting every kind so long as it did not transgress laws; thus showing that he was able, as every good citizen should be, to live under any form of constitution, while he refused to countenance illegality and was its constant enemy.

PART-29

So long as the fortune of the war continued even, the Athenians preserved the democracy; but after the disaster in Sicily, when the Lacedaemonians had gained the upper hand through their alliance with the king of Persia, they were compelled to abolish the democracy and establish in its place the constitution of the Four Hundred. The speech recommending this course before the vote was made by Melobius, and the motion was proposed by Pythodorus of Anaphlystus; but the real argument which persuaded the majority was the belief that the king of Persia was more likely to form an alliance with them if the constitution were on an oligarchical basis. The motion of Pythodorus was to the following effect. The popular Assembly was to elect twenty persons, over forty years of age, who, in conjunction with the existing ten members of the Committee of Public Safety, after taking an oath that they would frame such measures as they thought best for the state, should then prepare proposals for the public safety. In addition, any other person might make proposals, so that of all the schemes before them the people might choose the best. Cleitophon concurred with the motion of Pythodorus, but moved that the committee should also investigate the ancient laws enacted by Cleisthenes when he created the democracy, in order that they might have these too before them and so be in a position to decide wisely; his suggestion being that the constitution of Cleisthenes was not really democratic, but closely akin to that of Solon. When the committee was elected, their first proposal was that the Prytanes should be compelled to put to the vote any motion that was offered on behalf of the public safety. Next they abolished all indictments for illegal proposals, all impeachments and pubic prosecutions, in order that every Athenian should be free to give his counsel on the situation, if he chose; and they decreed that if any person imposed a fine on any other for his acts in this respect, or prosecuted him or summoned him before the courts, he should, on an information being laid against him, be summarily arrested and brought before the generals, who should deliver him to the Eleven to be put to death. After these preliminary measures, they drew up the constitution in the following manner. The revenues of the state were not to be spent on any purpose except the war. All magistrates should serve without remuneration for the period of the war, except the nine Archons and the Prytanes for the time being, who should each receive three obols a day. The whole of the rest of the administration was to be committed, for the period of the war, to those Athenians who were most capable of serving the state personally or pecuniarily, to the number of not less than five thousand. This body was to have full powers, to the extent even of making treaties with whomsoever they willed; and ten representatives, over forty years of age, were to be elected from each tribe to draw up the list of the Five Thousand, after taking an oath on a full and perfect sacrifice.

PART-30

THESE were the recommendations of the committee; and when they had been ratified the Five Thousand elected from their own number a hundred commissioners to draw up the constitution. They, on their appointment, drew up and produced the following recommendations. There should be a Council, holding office for a year, consisting of men over thirty years of age, serving without pay. To this body should belong the Generals, the nine Archons, the Amphictyonic Registrar (Hieromnemon), the Taxiarchs, the Hipparchs, the Phylarch, the commanders of garrisons, the Treasurers of Athena and the other gods, ten in number, the Hellenic Treasurers (Hellenotamiae), the Treasurers of the other non-sacred moneys, to the number of twenty, the ten Commissioners of Sacrifices (Hieropoei), and the ten Superintendents of the mysteries. All these were to be appointed by the Council from a larger number of selected candidates, chosen from its members for the time being. The other offices were all to be filled by lot, and not from the members of the Council. The Hellenic Treasurers who actually administered the funds should not sit with the Council. As regards the future, four Councils were to be created, of men of the age already mentioned, and one of these was to be chosen by lot to take office at once, while the others were to receive it in turn, in the order decided by the lot. For this purpose the hundred commissioners were to distribute themselves and all the rest as equally as possible into four parts, and cast lots for precedence, and the selected body should hold office for a year. They were to administer that office as seemed to them best, both with reference to the safe custody and due expenditure of the finances, and generally with regard to all other matters to the best of their ability. If they desired to take a larger number of persons into counsel, each member might call in one assistant of his own choice, subject to the same qualification of age. The Council was to sit once every five days, unless there was any special need for more frequent sittings. The casting of the lot for the Council was to be held by the nine Archons; votes on divisions were to be counted by five tellers chosen by lot from the members of the Council, and of these one was to be selected by lot every day to act as president. These five persons were to cast lots for precedence between the parties wishing to appear before the Council, giving the first place to sacred matters, the second to heralds, the third to embassies, and the fourth to all other subjects; but matters concerning the war might be dealt with, on the motion of the generals, whenever there was need, without balloting. Any member of the Council who did not enter the Council-house at the time named should be fined a drachma for each day, unless he was away on leave of absence from the Council.

PART-31

SUCH was the constitution which they drew up for the time to come, but for the immediate present they devised the following scheme. There should be a Council of Four Hundred, as in the ancient constitution, forty from each tribe, chosen out of candidates of more than thirty years of age, selected by the members of the tribes. This Council should appoint the magistrates and draw up the form of oath which they were to take; and in all that concerned the laws, in the examination of official accounts, and in other matters generally, they might act according to their discretion. They must, however, observe the laws that might be enacted with reference to the constitution of the state, and had no power to alter them nor to pass others. The generals should be provisionally elected from the whole body of the Five Thousand, but so soon as the Council came into existence it was to hold an examination of military equipments, and thereon elect ten persons, together with a secretary, and the persons thus elected should hold office during the coming year with full powers, and should have the right, whenever they desired it, of joining in the deliberations of the Council. The Five thousand was also to elect a single Hipparch and ten Phylarchs; but for the future the Council was to elect these officers according to the regulations above laid down. No office, except those of member of the Council and of general, might be held more than once, either by the first occupants or by their successors. With reference to the future distribution of the Four Hundred into the four successive sections, the hundred commissioners must divide them whenever the time comes for the citizens to join in the Council along with the rest.

PART-32

THE hundred commissioners appointed by the Five Thousand drew up the constitution as just stated; and after it had been ratified by the people, under the presidency of Aristomachus, the existing Council, that of the year of Callias, was dissolved before it had completed its term of office. It was dissolved on the fourteenth day of the month Thargelion, and the Four Hundred entered into office on the twenty-first; whereas the regular Council, elected by lot, ought to have entered into office on the fourteenth of Scirophorion. Thus was the oligarchy established, in the archonship of Callias, just about a hundred years after the expulsion of the tyrants. The chief promoters of the revolution were Pisander, Antiphon, and Theramenes, all of them men of good birth and with high reputations for ability and judgement. When, however, this constitution had been established, the Five Thousand were only nominally selected, and the Four Hundred, together with the ten officers on whom full powers had been conferred, occupied the Council-house and really administered the government. They began by sending ambassadors to the Lacedaemonians proposing a cessation of the war on the basis of the existing position; but as the Lacedaemonians refused to listen to them unless they would also abandon the command of the sea, they broke off the negotiations.

PART-33

FOR about four months the constitution of the Four Hundred lasted, and Mnasilochus held office as Archon of their nomination for two months of the year of Theopompus, who was Archon for the remaining ten. On the loss of the naval battle of Eretria, however, and the revolt of the whole of Euboea except Oreum, the indignation of the people was greater than at any of the earlier disasters, since they drew far more supplies at this time from Euboea than from Attica itself. Accordingly they deposed the Four Hundred and committed the management of affairs to the Five Thousand, consisting of persons possessing a military equipment. At the same time they voted that pay should not be given for any public office. The persons chiefly responsible for the revolution were Aristocrates and Theramenes, who disapproved of the action of the Four Hundred in retaining the direction of affairs entirely in their own hands, and referring nothing to the Five Thousand. During this period the constitution of the state seems to have been admirable, since it was a time of war and the franchise was in the hands of those who possessed a military equipment.

PART-34

THE people, however, in a very short time deprived the Five Thousand of their monopoly of the government. Then, six years after the overthrow of the Four Hundred, in the archonship of Callias of Angele, the battle of Arginusae took place, of which the results were, first, that the ten generals who had gained the victory were all condemned by a single decision, owing to the people being led astray by persons who aroused their indignation; though, as a matter of fact, some of the generals had actually taken no part in the battle, and others were themselves picked up by other vessels. Secondly, when the Lacedaemonians proposed to evacuate Decelea and make peace on the basis of the existing position, although some of the Athenians supported this proposal, the majority refused to listen to them. In this they were led astray by Cleophon, who appeared in the Assembly drunk and wearing his breastplate, and prevented peace being made, declaring that he would never accept peace unless the Lacedaemonians abandoned their claims on all the cities allied with them. They mismanaged their opportunity then, and in a very short time they learnt their mistake. The next year, in the archonship of Alexias, they suffered the disaster of Aegospotami, the consequence of which was that Lysander became master of the city, and set up the Thirty as its governors. He did so in the following manner. One of the terms of peace stipulated that the state should be governed according to 'the ancient constitution'. Accordingly the popular party tried to preserve the democracy, while that part of the upper class which belonged to the political clubs, together with the exiles who had returned since the peace, aimed at an oligarchy, and those who were not members of any club, though in other respects they considered themselves as good as any other citizens, were anxious to restore the ancient constitution. The latter class included Archinus, Anytus, Cleitophon, Phormisius, and many others, but their most prominent leader was Theramenes. Lysander, however, threw his influence on the side of the oligarchical party, and the popular Assembly was compelled by sheer intimidation to pass a vote establishing the oligarchy. The motion to this effect was proposed by Dracontides of Aphidna.

PART-35

IN this way were the Thirty established in power, in the archonship of Pythodorus. As soon, however, as they were masters of the city, they ignored all the resolutions which had been passed relating to the organization of the constitution, but after appointing a Council of Five Hundred and the other magistrates out of a thousand selected candidates, and associating with themselves ten Archons in Piraeus, eleven superintendents of the prison, and three hundred 'lash-bearers' as attendants, with the help of these they kept the city under their own control. At first, indeed, they behaved with moderation towards the citizens and pretended to administer the state according to the ancient constitution. In pursuance of this policy they took down from the hill of Areopagus the laws of Ephialtes and Archestratus relating to the Areopagite Council; they also repealed such of the statutes of Solon as were obscure, and abolished the supreme power of the law-courts. In this they claimed to be restoring the constitution and freeing it from obscurities; as, for instance, by making the testator free once for all to leave his property as he pleased, and abolishing the existing limitations in cases of insanity, old age, and undue female influence, in order that no opening might be left for professional accusers. In other matters also their conduct was similar. At first, then, they acted on these lines, and they destroyed the professional accusers and those mischievous and evil-minded persons who, to the great detriment of the democracy, had attached themselves to it in order to curry favour with it. With all of this the city was much pleased, and thought that the Thirty were doing it with the best of motives. But so soon as they had got a firmer hold on the city, they spared no class of citizens, but put to death any persons who were eminent for wealth or birth or character. Herein they aimed at removing all whom they had reason to fear, while they also wished to lay hands on their possessions; and in a short time they put to death not less than fifteen hundred persons.

PART-36

THERAMENES, however, seeing the city thus falling into ruin, was displeased with their proceedings, and counselled them to cease such unprincipled conduct and let the better classes have a share in the government. At first they resisted his advice, but when his proposals came to be known abroad, and the masses began to associate themselves with him, they were seized with alarm lest he should make himself the leader of the people and destroy their despotic power. Accordingly they drew up a list of three thousand citizens, to whom they announced that they would give a share in the constitution. Theramenes, however, criticized this scheme also, first on the ground that, while proposing to give all respectable citizens a share in the constitution, they were actually giving it only to three thousand persons, as though all merit were confined within that number; and secondly because they were doing two inconsistent things, since they made the government rest on the basis of force, and yet made the governors inferior in strength to the governed. However, they took no notice of his criticisms, and for a long time put off the publication of the list of the Three Thousand and kept to themselves the names of those who had been placed upon it; and every time they did decide to publish it they proceeded to strike out some of those who had been included in it, and insert others who had been omitted.

PART-37

Now when winter had set in, Thrasybulus and the exiles occupied Phyle, and the force which the Thirty led out to attack them met with a reverse. Thereupon the Thirty decided to disarm the bulk of the population and to get rid of Theramenes; which they did in the following way. They introduced two laws into the Council, which they commanded it to pass; the first of them gave the Thirty absolute power to put to death any citizen who was not included in the list of the Three Thousand, while the second disqualified all persons from participation in the franchise who should have assisted in the demolition of the fort of Eetioneia, or have acted in any way against the Four Hundred who had organized the previous oligarchy. Theramenes had done both, and accordingly, when these laws were ratified, he became excluded from the franchise and the Thirty had full power to put him to death. Theramenes having been thus removed, they disarmed all the people except the Three Thousand, and in every respect showed a great advance in cruelty and crime. They also sent ambassadors to Lacedaemonian to blacken the character of Theramenes and to ask for help; and the Lacedaemonians, in answer to their appeal, sent Callibius as military governor with about seven hundred troops, who came and occupied the Acropolis.

PART-38

THESE events were followed by the occupation of Munichia by the exiles from Phyle, and their victory over the Thirty and their partisans. After the fight the party of the city retreated, and next day they held a meeting in the marketplace and deposed the Thirty, and elected ten citizens with full powers to bring the war to a termination. When, however, the Ten had taken over the government they did nothing towards the object for which they were elected, but sent envoys to Lacedaemonian to ask for help and to borrow money. Further, finding that the citizens who possessed the franchise were displeased at their proceedings, they were afraid lest they should be deposed, and consequently, in order to strike terror into them (in which design they succeeded), they arrested Demaretus, one of the most eminent citizens, and put him to death. This gave them a firm hold on the government, and they also had the support of Callibius and his Peloponnesians, together with several of the Knights; for some of the members of this class were the most zealous among the citizens to prevent the return of the exiles from Phyle. When, however, the party in Piraeus and Munichia began to gain the upper hand in the war, through the defection of the whole populace to them, the party in the city deposed the original Ten, and elected another Ten, consisting of men of the highest repute. Under their administration, and with their active and zealous cooperation, the treaty of reconciliation was made and the populace returned to the city. The most prominent members of this board were Rhinon of Paeania and Phayllus of Acherdus, who, even before the arrival of Pausanias, opened negotiations with the party in Piraeus, and after his arrival seconded his efforts to bring about the return of the exiles. For it was Pausanias, the king of the Lacedaemonians, who brought the peace and reconciliation to a fulfillment, in conjunction with the ten commissioners of arbitration who arrived later from Lacedaemonian, at his own earnest request. Rhinon and his colleagues received a vote of thanks for the goodwill shown by them to the people, and though they received their charge under an oligarchy and handed in their accounts under a democracy, no one, either of the party that had stayed in the city or of the exiles that had returned from the Piraeus, brought any complaint against them. On the contrary, Rhinon was immediately elected general on account of his conduct in this office.

PART-39

THIS reconciliation was effected in the archonship of Eucleides, on the following terms. All persons who, having remained in the city during the troubles, were now anxious to leave it, were to be free to settle at Eleusis, retaining their civil rights and possessing full and independent powers of self-government, and with the free enjoyment of their own personal property. The temple at Eleusis should be common ground for both parties, and should be under the superintendence of the Ceryces, and the Eumolpidae, according to primitive custom. The settlers at Eleusis should not be allowed to enter Athens, nor the people of Athens to enter Eleusis, except at the season of the mysteries, when both parties should be free from these restrictions. The secessionists should pay their share to the fund for the common defence out of their revenues, just like all the other Athenians. If any of the seceding party wished to take a house in Eleusis, the people would help them to obtain the consent of the owner; but if they could not come to terms, they should appoint three valuers on either side, and the owner should receive whatever price they should appoint. Of the inhabitants of Eleusis, those whom the secessionists wished to remain should be allowed to do so. The list of those who desired to secede should be made up within ten days after the taking of the oaths in the case of persons already in the country, and their actual departure should take place within twenty days; persons at present out of the country should have the same terms allowed to them after their return. No one who settled at Eleusis should be capable of holding any office in Athens until he should again register himself on the roll as a resident in the city. Trials for homicide, including all cases in which one party had either killed or wounded another, should be conducted according to ancestral practice. There should be a general amnesty concerning past events towards all persons except the Thirty, the Ten, the Eleven, and the magistrates in Piraeus; and these too should be included if they should submit their accounts in the usual way. Such accounts should be given by the magistrates in Piraeus before a court of citizens rated in Piraeus, and by the magistrates in the city before a court of those rated in the city. On these terms those who wished to do so might secede. Each party was to repay separately the money which it had borrowed for the war.

PART-40

WHEN the reconciliation had taken place on these terms, those who had fought on the side of the Thirty felt considerable apprehensions, and a large number intended to secede. But as they put off entering their names till the last moment, as people will do, Archinus, observing their numbers, and being anxious to retain them as citizens, cut off the remaining days during which the list should have remained open; and in this way many persons were compelled to remain, though they did so very unwillingly until they recovered confidence. This is one point in which Archinus appears to have acted in a most statesmanlike manner, and another was his subsequent prosecution of Thrasybulus on the charge of illegality, for a motion by which he proposed to confer the franchise on all who had taken part in the return from Piraeus, although some of them were notoriously slaves. And yet a third such action was when one of the returned exiles began to violate the amnesty, whereupon Archinus haled him to the Council and persuaded them to execute him without trial, telling them that now they would have to show whether they wished to preserve the democracy and abide by the oaths they had taken; for if they let this man escape they would encourage others to imitate him, while if they executed him they would make an example for all to learn by. And this was exactly what happened; for after this man had been put to death no one ever again broke the amnesty. On the contrary, the Athenians seem, both in public and in private, to have behaved in the most unprecedentedly admirable and public-spirited way with reference to the preceding troubles. Not only did they blot out all memory of former offences, but they even repaid to the Lacedaemonians out of the public purse the money which the Thirty had borrowed for the war, although the treaty required each party, the party of the city and the party of Piraeus, to pay its own debts separately. This they did because they thought it was a necessary first step in the direction of restoring harmony; but in other states, so far from the democratic parties making advances from their own possessions, they are rather in the habit of making a general redistribution of the land. A final reconciliation was made with the secessionists at Eleusis two years after the secession, in the archonship of Xenaenetus.

PART-41

THIS, however, took place at a later date; at the time of which we are speaking the people, having secured the control of the state, established the constitution which exists at the present day. Pythodorus was Archon at the time, but the democracy seems to have assumed the supreme power with perfect justice, since it had effected its own return by its own exertions. This was the eleventh change which had taken place in the constitution of Athens. The first modification of the primaeval condition of things was when Ion and his companions brought the people together into a community, for then the people was first divided into the four tribes, and the tribe-kings were created. Next, and first after this, having now some semblance of a constitution, was that which took place in the reign of Theseus, consisting in a slight deviation from absolute monarchy. After this came the constitution formed under Draco, when the first code of laws was drawn up. The third was that which followed the civil war, in the time of Solon; from this the democracy took its rise. The fourth was the tyranny of Pisistratus; the fifth the constitution of Cleisthenes, after the overthrow of the tyrants, of a more democratic character than that of Solon. The sixth was that which followed on the Persian wars, when the Council of Areopagus had the direction of the state. The seventh, succeeding this, was the constitution which Aristides sketched out, and which Ephialtes brought to completion by overthrowing the Areopagite Council; under this the nation, misled by the demagogues, made the most serious mistakes in the interest of its maritime empire. The eighth was the establishment of the Four Hundred, followed by the ninth, the restored democracy. The tenth was the tyranny of the Thirty and the Ten. The eleventh was that which followed the return from Phyle and Piraeus; and this has continued from that day to this, with continual accretions of power to the masses. The democracy has made itself master of everything and administers everything by its votes in the Assembly and by the law-courts, in which it holds the supreme power. Even the jurisdiction of the Council has passed into the hands of the people at large; and this appears to be a judicious change, since small bodies are more open to corruption, whether by actual money or influence, than large ones. At first they refused to allow payment for attendance at the Assembly; but the result was that people did not attend. Consequently, after the Prytanes had tried many devices in vain in order to induce the populace to come and ratify the votes, Agyrrhius, in the first instance, made a provision of one obol a day, which Heracleides of Clazomenae, nicknamed 'the king', increased to two obols, and Agyrrhius again to three.

PART-42

THE present state of the constitution is as follows. The franchise is open to all who are of citizen birth by both parents. They are enrolled among the demesmen at the age of eighteen. On the occasion of their enrollment the demesmen give their votes on oath, first whether the candidates appear to be of the age prescribed by the law (if not, they are dismissed back into the ranks of the boys), and secondly whether the candidate is free born and of such parentage as the laws require. Then if they decide that he is not a free man, he appeals to the law-courts, and the demesmen appoint five of their own number to act as accusers; if the court decides that he has no right to be enrolled, he is sold by the state as a slave, but if he wins his case he has a right to be enrolled among the demesmen without further question. After this the Council examines those who have been enrolled, and if it comes to the conclusion that any of them is less than eighteen years of age, it fines the demesmen who enrolled him. When the youths (Ephebi) have passed this examination, their fathers meet by their tribes, and appoint on oath three of their fellow tribesmen, over forty years of age, who, in their opinion, are the best and most suitable persons to have charge of the youths; and of these the Assembly elects one from each tribe as guardian, together with a director, chosen from the general body of Athenians, to control the while. Under the charge of these persons the youths first of all make the circuit of the temples; then they proceed to Piraeus, and some of them garrison Munichia and some the south shore. The Assembly also elects two trainers, with subordinate instructors, who teach them to fight in heavy armour, to use the bow and javelin, and to discharge a catapult. The guardians receive from the state a drachma apiece for their keep, and the youths four obols apiece. Each guardian receives the allowance for all the members of his tribe and buys the necessary provisions for the common stock (they mess together by tribes), and generally superintends everything. In this way they spend the first year. The next year, after giving a public display of their military evolutions, on the occasion when the Assembly meets in the theatre, they receive a shield and spear from the state; after which they patrol the country and spend their time in the forts. For these two years they are on garrison duty, and wear the military cloak, and during this time they are exempt from all taxes. They also can neither bring an action at law, nor have one brought against them, in order that they may have no excuse for requiring leave of absence; though exception is made in cases of actions concerning inheritances and wards of state, or of any sacrificial ceremony connected with the family. When the two years have elapsed they thereupon take their position among the other citizens. Such is the manner of the enrollment of the citizens and the training of the youths.

PART-43

ALL the magistrates that are concerned with the ordinary routine of administration are elected by lot, except the Military Treasurer, the Commissioners of the Theoric fund, and the Superintendent of Springs. These are elected by vote, and hold office from one Panathenaic festival to the next. All military officers are also elected by vote.

The Council of Five Hundred is elected by lot, fifty from each tribe. Each tribe holds the office of Prytanes in turn, the order being determined by lot; the first four serve for thirty-six days each, the last six for thirty-five, since the reckoning is by lunar years. The Prytanes for the time being, in the first place, mess together in the Tholus, and receive a sum of money from the state for their maintenance; and, secondly, they convene the meetings of the Council and the Assembly. The Council they convene every day, unless it is a holiday, the Assembly four times in each prytany. It is also their duty to draw up the programme of the business of the Council and to decide what subjects are to be dealt with on each particular day, and where the sitting is to be held. They also draw up the programme for the meetings of the Assembly. One of these in each prytany is called the 'sovereign' Assembly; in this the people have to ratify the continuance of the magistrates in office, if they are performing their duties properly, and to consider the supply of corn and the defence of the country. On this day, too, impeachments are introduced by those who wish to do so, the lists of property confiscated by the state are read, and also applications for inheritances and wards of state, so that nothing may pass unclaimed without the cognizance of any person concerned. In the sixth prytany, in addition to the business already stated, the question is put to the vote whether it is desirable to hold a vote of ostracism or not; and complaints against professional accusers, whether Athenian or aliens domiciled in Athens, are received, to the number of not more than three of either class, together with cases in which an individual has made some promise to the people and has not performed it. Another Assembly in each prytany is assigned to the hearing of petitions, and at this meeting any one is free, on depositing the petitioner's olive-branch, to speak to the people concerning any matter, public or private. The two remaining meetings are devoted to all other subjects, and the laws require them to deal with three questions connected with religion, three connected with heralds and embassies, and three on secular subjects. Sometimes questions are brought forward without a preliminary vote of the Assembly to take them into consideration.

Heralds and envoys appear first before the Prytanes, and the bearers of dispatches also deliver them to the same officials.

PART-44

THERE is a single President of the Prytanes, elected by lot, who presides for a night and a day; he may not hold the office for more than that time, nor may the same individual hold it twice. He keeps the keys of the sanctuaries in which the treasures and public records of the state are preserved, and also the public seal; and he is bound to remain in the Tholus, together with one-third of the Prytanes, named by himself. Whenever the Prytanes convene a meeting of the Council or Assembly, he appoints by lot nine Proedri, one from each tribe except that which holds the office of Prytanes for the time being; and out of these nine he similarly appoints one as President, and hands over the programme for the meeting to them. They take it and see to the preservation of order, put forward the various subjects which are to be considered, decide the results of the votings, and direct the proceedings generally. They also have power to dismiss the meeting. No one may act as President more than once in the year, but he may be a Proedrus once in each prytany.

Elections to the offices of General and Hipparch and all other military commands are held in the Assembly, in such manner as the people decide; they are held after the sixth prytany by the first board of Prytanes in whose term of office the omens are favourable. There has, however, to be a preliminary consideration by the Council in this case also.

PART-45

IN former times the Council had full powers to inflict fines and imprisonment and death; but when it had consigned Lysimachus to the executioner, and he was sitting in the immediate expectation of death, Eumelides of Alopece rescued him from its hands, maintaining that no citizen ought to be put to death except on the decision of a court of law. Accordingly a trial was held in a law-court, and Lysimachus was acquitted, receiving henceforth the nickname of 'the man from the drum-head'; and the people deprived the Council thenceforward of the power to inflict death or imprisonment or fine, passing a law that if the Council condemn any person for an offence or inflict a fine, the Thesmothetae shall bring the sentence or fine before the law-court, and the decision of the jurors shall be the final judgement in the matter.

The Council passes judgement on nearly all magistrates, especially those who have the control of money; its judgement, however, is not final, but is subject to an appeal to the lawcourts. Private individuals, also, may lay an information against any magistrate they please for not obeying the laws, but here too there is an appeal to the law-courts if the Council declare the charge proved. The Council also examines those who are to be its members for the ensuing year, and likewise the nine Archons. Formerly the Council had full power to reject candidates for office as unsuitable, but now they have an appeal to the law-courts. In all these matters, therefore, the Council has no final jurisdiction. It takes, however, preliminary cognizance of all matters brought before the Assembly, and the Assembly cannot vote on any question unless it has first been considered by the Council and placed on the programme by the Prytanes; since a person who carries a motion in the Assembly is liable to an action for illegal proposal on these grounds.

PART-46

THE Council also superintends the triremes that are already in existence, with their tackle and sheds, and builds new triremes or quadriremes, whichever the Assembly votes, with tackle and sheds to match. The Assembly appoints master-builders for the ships by vote; and if they do not hand them over completed to the next Council, the old Council cannot receive the customary donation--that being normally given to it during its successor's term of office. For the building of the triremes it appoints ten commissioners, chosen from its own members. The Council also inspects all public buildings, and if it is of opinion that the state is being defrauded, it reports the culprit to the Assembly, and on condemnation hands him over to the law-courts.

PART-47

THE Council also co-operates with other magistrates in most of their duties. First there are the treasurers of Athena, ten in number, elected by lot, one from each tribe. According to the law of Solon--which is still in force--they must be Pentacosiomedimni, but in point of fact the person on whom the lot falls holds the office even though he be quite a poor man. These officers take over charge of the statue of Athena, the figures of Victory, and all the other ornaments of the temple, together with the money, in the presence of the Council. Then there are the Commissioners for Public Contracts (Poletae), ten in number, one chosen by lot from each tribe, who farm out the public contracts. They lease the mines and taxes, in conjunction with the Military Treasurer and the Commissioners of the Theoric fund, in the presence of the Council, and grant, to the persons indicated by the vote of the Council, the mines which are let out by the state, including both the workable ones, which are let for three years, and those which are let under special agreements years. They also sell, in the presence of the Council, the property of those who have gone into exile from the court of the Areopagus, and of others whose goods have been confiscated, and the nine Archons ratify the contracts. They also hand over to the Council lists of the taxes which are farmed out for the year, entering on whitened tablets the name of the lessee and the amount paid. They make separate lists, first of those who have to pay their instalments in each prytany, on ten several tablets, next of those who pay thrice in the year, with a separate tablet for each instalment, and finally of those who pay in the ninth prytany. They also draw up a list of farms and dwellings which have been confiscated and sold by order of the courts; for these too come within their province. In the case of dwellings the value must be paid up in five years, and in that of farms, in ten. The instalments are paid in the ninth prytany. Further, the King-archon brings before the Council the leases of the sacred enclosures, written on whitened tablets. These too are leased for ten years, and the instalments are paid in the prytany; consequently it is in this prytany that the greatest amount of money is collected. The tablets containing the lists of the instalments are carried into the Council, and the public clerk takes charge of them. Whenever a payment of instalments is to be made he takes from the pigeon-holes the precise list of the sums which are to be paid and struck off on that day, and delivers it to the Receivers-General. The rest are kept apart, in order that no sum may be struck off before it is paid.

PART-48

THERE are ten Receivers-General (Apodectae), elected by lot, one from each tribe. These officers receive the tablets, and strike off the instalments as they are paid, in the presence of the Council in the Council-chamber, and give the tablets back to the public clerk. If any one fails to pay his instalment, a note is made of it on the tablet; and he is bound to pay double the amount of the deficiency, or, in default, to be imprisoned. The Council has full power by the laws to exact these payments and to inflict this imprisonment. They receive all the instalments, therefore, on one day, and portion the money out among the magistrates; and on the next day they bring up the report of the apportionment, written on a wooden notice-board, and read it out in the Council-chamber, after which they ask publicly in the Council whether any one knows of any malpractice in reference to the apportionment, on the part of either a magistrate or a private individual, and if any one is charged with malpractice they take a vote on it.

The Council also elects ten Auditors (Logistae) by lot from its own members, to audit the accounts of the magistrates for each prytany. They also elect one Examiner of Accounts (Euthunus) by lot from each tribe, with two assessors (Paredri) for each examiner, whose duty it is to sit at the ordinary market hours, each opposite the statue of the eponymous hero of his tribe; and if any one wishes to prefer a charge, on either public or private grounds, against any magistrate who has passed his audit before the law-courts, within three days of his having so passed, he enters on a whitened tablet his own name and that of the magistrate prosecuted, together with the malpractice that is alleged against him. He also appends his claim for a penalty of such amount as seems to him fitting, and gives in the record to the Examiner. The latter takes it, and if after reading it he considers it proved he hands it over, if a private case, to the local justices who introduce cases for the tribe concerned, while if it is a public case he enters it on the register of the Thesmothetae. Then, if the Thesmothetae accept it, they bring the accounts of this magistrate once more before the law-court, and the decision of the jury stands as the final judgement.

PART-49

THE Council also inspects the horses belonging to the state. If a man who has a good horse is found to keep it in bad condition, he is mulcted in his allowance of corn; while those which cannot keep up or which shy and will not stand steady, it brands with a wheel on the jaw, and the horse so marked is disqualified for service. It also inspects those who appear to be fit for service as scouts, and any one whom it rejects is deprived of his horse. It also examines the infantry who serve among the cavalry, and any one whom it rejects ceases to receive his pay. The roll of the cavalry is drawn up by the Commissioners of Enrolment (Catalogeis), ten in number, elected by the Assembly by open vote. They hand over to the Hipparchs and Phylarchs the list of those whom they have enrolled, and these officers take it and bring it up before the Council, and there open the sealed tablet containing the names of the cavalry. If any of those who have been on the roll previously make affidavit that they are physically incapable of cavalry service, they strike them out; then they call up the persons newly enrolled, and if any one makes affidavit that he is either physically or pecuniarily incapable of cavalry service they dismiss him, but if no such affidavit is made the Council vote whether the individual in question is suitable for the purpose or not. If they vote in the affirmative his name is entered on the tablet; if not, he is dismissed with the others.

Formerly the Council used to decide on the plans for public buildings and the contract for making the robe of Athena; but now this work is done by a jury in the law-courts appointed by lot, since the Council was considered to have shown favouritism in its decisions. The Council also shares with the Military Treasurer the superintendence of the manufacture of the images of Victory and the prizes at the Panathenaic festival.

The Council also examines infirm paupers; for there is a law which provides that persons possessing less than three minas, who are so crippled as to be unable to do any work, are, after examination by the Council, to receive two obols a day from the state for their support. A treasurer is appointed by lot to attend to them.

The Council also, speaking broadly, cooperates in most of the duties of all the other magistrates; and this ends the list of the functions of that body.

PART-50

THERE are ten Commissioners for Repairs of Temples, elected by lot, who receive a sum of thirty minas from the Receivers-General, and therewith carry out the most necessary repairs in the temples.

There are also ten City Commissioners (Astynomi), of whom five hold office in Piraeus and five in the city. Their duty is to see that female flute- and harp- and lute-players are not hired at more than two drachmas, and if more than one person is anxious to hire the same girl, they cast lots and hire her out to the person to whom the lot falls. They also provide that no collector of sewage shall shoot any of his sewage within ten stradia of the walls; they prevent people from blocking up the streets by building, or stretching barriers across them, or making drain-pipes in mid-air with a discharge into the street, or having doors which open outwards; they also remove the corpses of those who die in the streets, for which purpose they have a body of state slaves assigned to them.

PART-51

MARKET Commissioners (Agoranomi) are elected by lot, five for Piraeus, five for the city. Their statutory duty is to see that all articles offered for sale in the market are pure and unadulterated.

Commissioners of Weights and Measures (Metronomi) are elected by lot, five for the city, and five for Piraeus. They see that sellers use fair weights and measures.

Formerly there were ten Corn Commissioners (Sitophylaces), elected by lot, five for Piraeus, and five for the city; but now there are twenty for the city and fifteen for Piraeus. Their duties are, first, to see that the unprepared corn in the market is offered for sale at reasonable prices, and secondly, to see that the millers sell barley meal at a price proportionate to that of barley, and that the bakers sell their loaves at a price proportionate to that of wheat, and of such weight as the Commissioners may appoint; for the law requires them to fix the standard weight.

There are ten Superintendents of the Mart, elected by lot, whose duty is to superintend the Mart, and to compel merchants to bring up into the city two-thirds of the corn which is brought by sea to the Corn Mart.

PART-52

THE Eleven also are appointed by lot to take care of the prisoners in the state gaol. Thieves, kidnappers, and pickpockets are brought to them, and if they plead guilty they are executed, but if they deny the charge the Eleven bring the case before the law-courts; if the prisoners are acquitted, they release them, but if not, they then execute them. They also bring up before the law-courts the list of farms and houses claimed as state-property; and if it is decided that they are so, they deliver them to the Commissioners for Public Contracts. The Eleven also bring up informations laid against magistrates alleged to be disqualified; this function comes within their province, but some such cases are brought up by the Thesmothetae.

There are also five Introducers of Cases (Eisagogeis), elected by lot, one for each pair of tribes, who bring up the 'monthly' cases to the law-courts. 'Monthly' cases are these: refusal to pay up a dowry where a party is bound to do so, refusal to pay interest on money borrowed at 12 per cent., or where a man desirous of setting up business in the market has borrowed from another man capital to start with; also cases of slander, cases arising out of friendly loans or partnerships, and cases concerned with slaves, cattle, and the office of trierarch, or with banks. These are brought up as 'monthly' cases and are introduced by these officers; but the Receivers-General perform the same function in cases for or against the farmers of taxes. Those in which the sum concerned is not more than ten drachmas they can decide summarily, but all above that amount they bring into the law-courts as 'monthly' cases.

PART-53

THE Forty are also elected by lot, four from each tribe, before whom suitors bring all other cases. Formerly they were thirty in number, and they went on circuit through the demes to hear causes; but after the oligarchy of the Thirty they were increased to forty. They have full powers to decide cases in which the amount at issue does not exceed ten drachmas, but anything beyond that value they hand over to the

Arbitrators. The Arbitrators take up the case, and, if they cannot bring the parties to an agreement, they give a decision. If their decision satisfies both parties, and they abide by it, the case is at an end; but if either of the parties appeals to the law-courts, the Arbitrators enclose the evidence, the pleadings, and the laws quoted in the case in two urns, those of the plaintiff in the one, and those of the defendant in the other. These they seal up and, having attached to them the decision of the arbitrator, written out on a tablet, place them in the custody of the four justices whose function it is to introduce cases on behalf of the tribe of the defendant. These officers take them and bring up the case before the law-court, to a jury of two hundred and one members in cases up to the value of a thousand drachmas, or to one of four hundred and one in cases above that value. No laws or pleadings or evidence may be used except those which were adduced before the Arbitrator, and have been enclosed in the urns.

The Arbitrators are persons in the sixtieth year of their age; this appears from the schedule of the Archons and the Eponymi. There are two classes of Eponymi, the ten who give their names to the tribes, and the forty-two of the years of service. The youths, on being enrolled among the citizens, were formerly registered upon whitened tablets, and the names were appended of the Archon in whose year they were enrolled, and of the Eponymus who had been in course in the preceding year; at the present day they are written on a bronze pillar, which stands in front of the Council-chamber, near the Eponymi of the tribes. Then the Forty take the last of the Eponymi of the years of service, and assign the arbitrations to the persons belonging to that year, casting lots to determine which arbitrations each shall undertake; and every one is compelled to carry through the arbitrations which the lot assigns to him. The law enacts that any one who does not serve as Arbitrator when he has arrived at the necessary age shall lose his civil rights, unless he happens to be holding some other office during that year, or to be out of the country. These are the only persons who escape the duty. Any one who suffers injustice at the hands of the Arbitrator may appeal to the whole board of Arbitrators, and if they find the magistrate guilty, the law enacts that he shall lose his civil rights. The persons thus condemned have, however, in their turn an appeal. The Eponymi are also used in reference to military expeditions; when the men of military age are despatched on service, a notice is put up stating that the men from such-and-such an Archon and

Eponymus to such-and-such another Archon and Eponymus are to go on the expedition.

PART-54

THE following magistrates also are elected by lot: Five Commissioners of Roads (Hodopoei), who, with an assigned body of public slaves, are required to keep the roads in order: and ten Auditors, with ten assistants, to whom all persons who have held any office must give in their accounts. These are the only officers who audit the accounts of those who are subject to examination, and who bring them up for examination before the law-courts. If they detect any magistrate in embezzlement, the jury condemn him for theft, and he is obliged to repay tenfold the sum he is declared to have misappropriated. If they charge a magistrate with accepting bribes and the jury convict him, they fine him for corruption, and this sum too is repaid tenfold. Or if they convict him of unfair dealing, he is fined on that charge, and the sum assessed is paid without increase, if payment is made before the ninth prytany, but otherwise it is doubled. A tenfold fine is not doubled.

The Clerk of the prytany, as he is called, is also elected by lot. He has the charge of all public documents, and keeps the resolutions which are passed by the Assembly, and checks the transcripts of all other official papers and attends at the sessions of the Council. Formerly he was elected by open vote, and the most distinguished and trustworthy persons were elected to the post, as is known from the fact that the name of this officer is appended on the pillars recording treaties of alliance and grants of consulship and citizenship. Now, however, he is elected by lot. There is, in addition, a Clerk of the Laws, elected by lot, who attends at the sessions of the Council; and he too checks the transcript of all the laws. The Assembly also elects by open vote a clerk to read documents to it and to the Council; but he has no other duty except that of reading aloud.

The Assembly also elects by lot the Commissioners of Public Worship (Hieropoei) known as the Commissioners for Sacrifices, who offer the sacrifices appointed by oracle, and, in conjunction with the seers, take the auspices whenever there is occasion. It also elects by lot ten others, known as Annual Commissioners, who offer certain sacrifices and administer all the quadrennial festivals except the Panathenaea. There are the following quadrennial festivals: first that of Delos (where there is also a sexennial festival), secondly the Brauronia, thirdly the Heracleia, fourthly the Eleusinia, and fifthly the Panathenaea; and no two of these are celebrated in the same place. To these the Hephaestia has now been added, in the archonship of Cephisophon.

An Archon is also elected by lot for Salamis, and a Demarch for Piraeus. These officers celebrate the Dionysia in these two places, and appoint Choregi. In Salamis, moreover, the name of the Archon is publicly recorded.

PART-55

ALL the foregoing magistrates are elected by lot, and their powers are those which have been stated. To pass on to the nine Archons, as they are called, the manner of their appointment from the earliest times has been described already. At the present day six Thesmothetae are elected by lot, together with their clerk, and in addition to these an Archon, a King, and a Polemarch. One is elected from each tribe. They are examined first of all by the Council of Five Hundred, with the exception of the clerk. The latter is examined only in the lawcourt, like other magistrates (for all magistrates, whether elected by lot or by open vote, are examined before entering on their offices); but the nine Archons are examined both in the Council and again in the law-court. Formerly no one could hold the office if the Council rejected him, but now there is an appeal to the law-court, which is the final authority in the matter of the examination. When they are examined, they are asked, first, 'Who is your father, and of what deme? who is your father's father? who is your mother? who is your mother's father, and of what deme?' Then the candidate is asked whether he possesses an ancestral Apollo and a household Zeus, and where their sanctuaries are; next if he possesses a family tomb, and where; then if he treats his parents well, and pays his taxes, and has served on the required military expeditions. When the examiner has put these questions, he proceeds, 'Call the witnesses to these facts'; and when the candidate has produced his witnesses, he next asks, 'Does any one wish to make any accusation against this man?' If an accuser appears, he gives the parties an opportunity of making their accusation and defence, and then puts it to the Council to pass the candidate or not, and to the law-court to give the final vote. If no one wishes to make an accusation, he proceeds at once to the vote. Formerly a single individual gave the vote, but now all the members are obliged to vote on the candidates, so that if any unprincipled candidate has managed to get rid of his accusers, it may still be possible for him to be disqualified before the law-court. When the examination has been thus completed, they proceed to the stone on which are the pieces of the victims, and on which the Arbitrators take oath before declaring their decisions, and witnesses swear to their testimony. On this stone the Archons stand, and swear to execute their office uprightly and according to the laws, and not to receive presents in respect of the performance of their duties, or, if they do, to dedicate a golden statue. When they have taken this oath they proceed to the Acropolis, and there they repeat it; after this they enter upon their office.

PART-56

THE Archon, the King, and the Polemarch have each two assessors, nominated by themselves. These officers are examined in the lawcourt before they begin to act, and give in accounts on each occasion of their acting.

As soon as the Archon enters office, he begins by issuing a proclamation that whatever any one possessed before he entered into office, that he shall possess and hold until the end of his term. Next he assigns Choregi to the tragic poets, choosing three of the richest persons out of the whole body of Athenians. Formerly he used also to assign five Choregi to the comic poets, but now the tribes provide the Choregi for them. Then he receives the Choregi who have been appointed by the tribes for the men's and boys' choruses and the comic poets at the Dionysia, and for the men's and boys' choruses at the Thargelia (at the Dionysia there is a chorus for each tribe, but at the Thargelia one between two tribes, each tribe bearing its share in providing it); he transacts the exchanges of properties for them, and reports any excuses that are tendered, if any one says that he has already borne this burden, or that he is exempt because he has borne a similar burden and the period of his exemption has not yet expired, or that he is not of the required age; since the Choregus of a boys' chorus must be over forty years of age. He also appoints Choregi for the festival at Delos, and a chief of the mission for the thirty-oar boat which conveys the youths thither. He also superintends sacred processions, both that in honour of Asclepius, when the initiated keep house, and that of the great Dionysia--the latter in conjunction with the Superintendents of that festival. These officers, ten in number, were formerly elected by open vote in the Assembly, and used to provide for the expenses of the procession out of their private means; but now one is elected by lot from each tribe, and the state contributes a hundred minas for the expenses. The Archon also superintends the procession at the Thargelia, and that in honour of Zeus the Saviour. He also manages the contests at the Dionysia and the Thargelia.

These, then, are the festivals which he superintends. The suits and indictments which come before him, and which he, after a preliminary inquiry, brings up before the lawcourts, are as follows. Injury to parents (for bringing these actions the prosecutor cannot suffer any penalty); injury to orphans (these actions lie against their guardians); injury to a ward of state (these lie against their guardians or their husbands), injury to an orphan's estate (these too lie against the guardians); mental derangement, where a party charges another with destroying his own property through unsoundness of mind; for appointment of liquidators, where a party refuses to divide property in which others have a share; for constituting a wardship; for determining between rival claims to a wardship; for granting inspection of property to which another party lays claim; for appointing oneself as guardian; and for determining disputes as to inheritances and wards of state. The Archon also has the care of orphans and wards of state, and of women who, on the death of their husbands, declare themselves to be with child; and he has power to inflict a fine on those who offend against the persons under his charge, or to bring the case before the law-courts. He also leases the houses of orphans and wards of state until they reach the age of fourteen, and takes mortgages on them; and if the guardians fail to provide the necessary food for the children under their charge, he exacts it from them. Such are the duties of the Archon.

PART-57

THE King in the first place superintends the mysteries, in conjunction with the Superintendents of Mysteries. The latter are elected in the Assembly by open vote, two from the general body of Athenians, one from the Eumolpidae, and one from the Ceryces. Next, he superintends the Lenaean Dionysia, which consists of a procession and a contest. The procession is ordered by the King and the Superintendents in conjunction; but the contest is managed by the King alone. He also manages all the contests of the torch-race; and to speak broadly, he administers all the ancestral sacrifices. Indictments for impiety come before him, or any disputes between parties concerning priestly rites; and he also determines all controversies concerning sacred rites for the ancient families and the priests. All actions for homicide come before him, and it is he that makes the proclamation requiring polluted persons to keep away from sacred ceremonies. Actions for homicide and wounding are heard, if the homicide or wounding be willful, in the Areopagus; so also in cases of killing by poison, and of arson. These are the only cases heard by that Council. Cases of unintentional homicide, or of intent to kill, or of killing a slave or a resident alien or a foreigner, are heard by the court of Palladium. When the homicide is acknowledged, but legal justification is pleaded, as when a man takes an adulterer in the act, or kills another by mistake in battle, or in an athletic contest, the prisoner is tried in the court of Delphinium. If a man who is in banishment for a homicide which admits of reconciliation incurs a further charge of killing or wounding, he is tried in Phreatto, and he makes his defence from a boat moored near the shore. All these cases, except those which are heard in the Areopagus, are tried by the Ephetae on whom the lot falls. The King introduces them, and the hearing is held within sacred precincts and in the open air. Whenever the King hears a case he takes off his crown. The person who is charged with homicide is at all other times excluded from the temples, nor is it even lawful for him to enter the market-place; but on the occasion of his trial he enters the temple and makes his defence. If the actual offender is unknown, the writ runs against 'the doer of the deed'. The King and the tribe-kings also hear the cases in which the guilt rests on inanimate objects and the lower animal.

PART-58

THE Polemarch performs the sacrifices to Artemis the huntress and to Enyalius, and arranges the contest at the funeral of those who have fallen in war, and makes offerings to the memory of Harmodius and Aristogeiton. Only private actions come before him, namely those in which resident aliens, both ordinary and privileged, and agents of foreign states are concerned. It is his duty to receive these cases and divide them into ten groups, and assign to each tribe the group which comes to it by lot; after which the magistrates who introduce cases for the tribe hand them over to the Arbitrators. The Polemarch, however, brings up in person cases in which an alien is charged with deserting his patron or neglecting to provide himself with one, and also of inheritances and wards of state where aliens are concerned; and in fact, generally, whatever the Archon does for citizens, the Polemarch does for aliens.

PART-59

THE Thesmothetae in the first place have the power of prescribing on what days the lawcourts are to sit, and next of assigning them to the several magistrates; for the latter must follow the arrangement which the Thesmothetae assign. Moreover they introduce impeachments before the Assembly, and bring up all votes for removal from office, challenges of a magistrate's conduct before the Assembly, indictments for illegal proposals, or for proposing a law which is contrary to the interests of the state, complaints against Proedri or their president for their conduct in office, and the accounts presented by the generals. All indictments also come before them in which a deposit has to be made by the prosecutor, namely, indictments for concealment of foreign origin, for corrupt evasion of foreign origin (when a man escapes the disqualification by bribery), for blackmailing accusations, bribery, false entry of another as a state debtor, false testimony to the service of a summons, conspiracy to enter a man as a state debtor, corrupt removal from the list of debtors, and adultery. They also bring up the examinations of all magistrates, and the rejections by the demes and the condemnations by the Council. Moreover they bring up certain private suits in cases of merchandise and mines, or where a slave has slandered a free man. It is they also who cast lots to assign the courts to the various magistrates, whether for private or public cases. They ratify commercial treaties, and bring up the cases which arise out of such treaties; and they also bring up cases of perjury from the Areopagus. The casting of lots for the jurors is conducted by all the nine Archons, with the clerk to the Thesmothetae as the tenth, each performing the duty for his own tribe. Such are the duties of the nine Archons.

PART-60

THERE are also ten Commissioners of Games (Athlothetae), elected by lot, one from each tribe. These officers, after passing an examination, serve for four years; and they manage the Panathenaic procession, the contest in music and that in gymnastic, and the horse-race; they also provide the robe of Athena and, in conjunction with the Council, the vases, and they present the oil to the athletes. This oil is collected from the sacred olives. The Archon requisitions it from the owners of the farms on which the sacred olives grow, at the rate of three-quarters of a pint from each plant. Formerly the state used to sell the fruit itself, and if any one dug up or broke down one of the sacred olives, he was tried by the Council of Areopagus, and if he was condemned, the penalty was death. Since, however, the oil has been paid by the owner of the farm, the procedure has lapsed, though the law remains; and the oil is a state charge upon the property instead of being taken from the individual plants. When, then, the Archon has collected the oil for his year of office, he hands it over to the Treasurers to preserve in the Acropolis, and he may not take his seat in the Areopagus until he has paid over to the Treasurers the full amount. The Treasurers keep it in the Acropolis until the Panathenaea, when they measure it out to the Commissioners of Games, and they again to the victorious competitors. The prizes for the victors in the musical contest consist of silver and gold, for the victors in manly vigour, of shields, and for the victors in the gymnastic contest and the horse-race, of oil.

PART-61

ALL officers connected with military service are elected by open vote. In the first place, ten Generals (Strategi), who were formerly elected one from each tribe, but now are chosen from the whole mass of citizens. Their duties are assigned to them by open vote; one is appointed to command the heavy infantry, and leads them if they go out to war; one to the defence of the country, who remains on the defensive, and fights if there is war within the borders of the country; two to Piraeus, one of whom is assigned to Munichia, and one to the south shore, and these have charge of the defence of the Piraeus; and one to superintend the symmories, who nominates the trierarchs arranges exchanges of properties for them, and brings up actions to decide on rival claims in connexion with them. The rest are dispatched to whatever business may be on hand at the moment. The appointment of these officers is submitted for confirmation in each prytany, when the question is put whether they are considered to be doing their duty. If any officer is rejected on this vote, he is tried in the lawcourt, and if he is found guilty the people decide what punishment or fine shall be inflicted on him; but if he is acquitted he resumes his office. The Generals have full power, when on active service, to arrest any one for insubordination, or to cashier him publicly, or to inflict a fine; the latter is, however, unusual.

There are also ten Taxiarchs, one from each tribe, elected by open vote; and each commands his own tribesmen and appoints captains of companies (Lochagi). There are also two Hipparchs, elected by open vote from the whole mass of the citizens, who command the cavalry, each taking five tribes. They have the same powers as the Generals have in respect of the infantry, and their appointments are also subject to confirmation. There are also ten Phylarchs, elected by open vote, one from each tribe, to command the cavalry, as the Taxiarchs do the infantry. There is also a Hipparch for Lemnos, elected by open vote, who has charge of the cavalry in Lemnos. There is also a treasurer of the Paralus, and another of the Ammonias, similarly elected.

PART-62

OF the magistrates elected by lot, in former times some including the nine Archons, were elected out of the tribe as a whole, while others, namely those who are now elected in the Theseum, were apportioned among the demes; but since the demes used to sell the elections, these magistrates too are now elected from the whole tribe, except the members of the Council and the guards of the dockyards, who are still left to the demes.

Pay is received for the following services. First the members of the Assembly receive a drachma for the ordinary meetings, and nine obols for the 'sovereign' meeting. Then the jurors at the law-courts receive three obols; and the members of the Council five obols. The Prytanes receive an allowance of an obol for their maintenance. The nine Archons receive four obols apiece for maintenance, and also keep a herald and a flute-player; and the Archon for Salamis receives a drachma a day. The Commissioners for Games dine in the Prytaneum during the month of Hecatombaeon in which the Panathenaic festival takes place, from the fourteenth day onwards. The Amphictyonic deputies to Delos receive a drachma a day from the exchequer of Delos. Also all magistrates sent to Samos, Scyros, Lemnos, or Imbros receive an allowance for their maintenance. The military offices may be held any number of times, but none of the others more than once, except the membership of the Council, which may be held twice.

PART-63

The juries for the law-courts are chosen by lot by the nine Archons, each for their own tribe, and by the clerk to the Thesmothetae for the tenth. There are ten entrances into the courts, one for each tribe; twenty rooms in which the lots are drawn, two for each tribe; a hundred chests, ten for each tribe; other chests, in which are placed the tickets of the jurors on whom the lot falls; and two vases. Further, staves, equal in number to the jurors required, are placed by the side of each entrance; and counters are put into one vase, equal in number to the staves. These are inscribed with letters of the alphabet beginning with the eleventh (lambda), equal in number to the courts which require to be filled. All persons above thirty years of age are qualified to serve as jurors, provided they are not debtors to the state and have not lost their civil rights. If any unqualified person serves as juror, an information is laid against him, and he is brought before the court; and, if he is convicted, the jurors assess the punishment or fine which they consider him to deserve. If he is condemned to a money fine, he must be imprisoned until he has paid up both the original debt, on account of which the information was laid against him, and also the fine which the court as imposed upon him. Each juror has his ticket of boxwood, on which is inscribed his name, with the name of his father and his deme, and one of the letters of the alphabet up to kappa; for the jurors in their several tribes are divided into ten sections, with approximately an equal number in each letter. When the Thesmothetes has decided by lot which letters are required to attend at the courts, the servant puts up above each court the letter which has been assigned to it by the lot.

PART-64

The ten chests above mentioned are placed in front of the entrance used by each tribe, and are inscribed with the letters of the alphabet from alpha to kappa. The jurors cast in their tickets, each into the chest on which is inscribed the letter which is on his ticket; then the servant shakes them all up, and the Archon draws one ticket from each chest. The individual so selected is called the Ticket-hanger (Empectes), and his function is to hang up the tickets out of his chest on the bar which bears the same letter as that on the chest. He is chosen by lot, lest, if the Ticket-hanger were always the same person, he might tamper with the results.

There are five of these bars in each of the rooms assigned for the lot-drawing. Then the Archon casts in the dice and thereby chooses the jurors from each tribe, room by room. The dice are made of brass, coloured black or white; and according to the number of jurors required, so many white dice are put in, one for each five tickets, while the remainder are black, in the same proportion. As the Archon draws out the dice, the crier calls out the names of the individuals chosen. The Ticket-hanger is included among those selected. Each juror, as he is chosen and answers to his name, draws a counter from the vase, and holding it out with the letter uppermost shows it first to the presiding Archon; and he, when he has seen it, throws the ticket of the juror into the chest on which is inscribed the letter which is on the counter, so that the juror must go into the court assigned to him by lot, and not into one chosen by himself, and that it may be impossible for any one to collect the jurors of his choice into any particular court. For this purpose chests are placed near the Archon, as many in number as there are courts to be filled that day, bearing the letters of the courts on which the lot has fallen.

PART-65

THE juror thereupon, after showing his counter again to the attendant, passes through the barrier into the court. The attendant gives him a staff of the same colour as the court bearing the letter which is on his counter, so as to ensure his going into the court assigned to him by lot; since, if he were to go into any other, he would be betrayed by the colour of his staff. Each court has a certain colour painted on the lintel of the entrance. Accordingly the juror, bearing his staff, enters the court which has the same colour as his staff, and the same letter as his counter. As he enters, he receives a voucher from the official to whom this duty has been assigned by lot. So with their counters and their staves the selected jurors take their seats in the court, having thus completed the process of admission. The unsuccessful candidates receive back their tickets from the Ticket-hangers. The public servants carry the chests from each tribe, one to each court, containing the names of the members of the tribe who are in that court, and hand them over to the officials assigned to the duty of giving back their tickets to the jurors in each court, so that these officials may call them up by name and pay them their fee.

PART-66

WHEN all the courts are full, two ballot boxes are placed in the first court, and a number of brazen dice, bearing the colours of the several courts, and other dice inscribed with the names of the presiding magistrates. Then two of the Thesmothetae, selected by lot, severally throw the dice with the colours into one box, and those with the magistrates' names into the other. The magistrate whose name is first drawn is thereupon proclaimed by the crier as assigned for duty in the court which is first drawn, and the second in the second, and similarly with the rest. The object of this procedure is that no one may know which court he will have, but that each may take the court assigned to him by lot.

When the jurors have come in, and have been assigned to their respective courts, the presiding magistrate in each court draws one ticket out of each chest (making ten in all, one out of each tribe), and throws them into another empty chest. He then draws out five of them, and assigns one to the superintendence of the water-clock, and the other four to the telling of the votes. This is to prevent any tampering beforehand with either the superintendent of the clock or the tellers of the votes, and to secure that there is no malpractice in these respects. The five who have not been selected for these duties receive from them a statement of the order in which the jurors shall receive their fees, and of the places where the several tribes shall respectively gather in the court for this purpose when their duties are completed; the object being that the jurors may be broken up into small groups for the reception of their pay, and not all crowd together and impede one another.

PART-67

THESE preliminaries being concluded, the cases are called on. If it is a day for private cases, the private litigants are called. Four cases are taken in each of the categories defined in the law, and the litigants swear to confine their speeches to the point at issue. If it is a day for public causes, the public litigants are called, and only one case is tried. Water-clocks are provided, having small supply-tubes, into which the water is poured by which the length of the pleadings is regulated. Ten gallons are allowed for a case in which an amount of more than five thousand drachmas is involved, and three for the second speech on each side.

When the amount is between one and five thousand drachmas, seven gallons are allowed for the first speech and two for the second; when it is less than one thousand, five and two. Six gallons are allowed for arbitrations between rival claimants, in which there is no second speech. The official chosen by lot to superintend the water-clock places his hand on the supply tube whenever the clerk is about to read a resolution or law or affidavit or treaty. When, however, a case is conducted according to a set measurement of the day, he does not stop the supply, but each party receives an equal allowance of water. The standard of measurement is the length of the days in the month Poseideon. The measured day is employed in cases when imprisonment, death, exile, loss of civil rights, or confiscation of goods is assigned as the penalty.

PART-68

MOST of the courts consist of 500 members; and when it is necessary to bring public cases before a jury of 1,000 members, two courts combine for the purpose, the most important cases of all are brought 1,500 jurors, or three courts. The ballot balls are made of brass with stems running through the centre, half of them having the stem pierced and the other half solid. When the speeches are concluded, the officials assigned to the taking of the votes give each juror two ballot balls, one pierced and one solid. This is done in full view of the rival litigants, to secure that no one shall receive two pierced or two solid balls. Then the official designated for the purpose takes away the jurors' staves, in return for which each one as he records his vote receives a brass voucher marked with the numeral 3 (because he gets three obols when he gives it up). This is to ensure that all shall vote; since no one can get a voucher unless he votes. Two urns, one of brass and the other of wood, stand in the court, in distinct spots so that no one may surreptitiously insert ballot balls; in these the jurors record their votes. The brazen urn is for effective votes, the wooden for unused votes; and the brazen urn has a lid pierced so as to take only one ballot ball, in order that no one may put in two at a time.

When the jurors are about to vote, the crier demands first whether the litigants enter a protest against any of the evidence; for no protest can be received after the voting has begun. Then he proclaims again, 'The pierced ballot for the plaintiff, the solid for the defendant'; and the juror, taking his two ballot balls from the stand, with his hand closed over the stem so as not to show either the pierced or the solid ballot to the litigants, casts the one which is to count into the brazen urn, and the other into the wooden urn.

PART-69

WHEN all the jurors have voted, the attendants take the urn containing the effective votes and discharge them on to a reckoning board having as many cavities as there are ballot balls, so that the effective votes, whether pierced or solid, may be plainly displayed and easily counted. Then the officials assigned to the taking of the votes tell them off on the board, the solid in one place and the pierced in another, and the crier announces the numbers of the votes, the pierced ballots being for the prosecutor and the solid for the defendant. Whichever has the majority is victorious; but if the votes are equal the verdict is for the defendant. Each juror receives two ballots, and uses one to record his vote, and throws the other away.

Then, if damages have to be awarded, they vote again in the same way, first returning their pay-vouchers and receiving back their staves. Half a gallon of water is allowed to each party for the discussion of the damages. Finally, when all has been completed in accordance with the law, the jurors receive their pay in the order assigned by the lot.

THE END

www.ingramcontent.com/pod-product-compliance
Lightning Source LLC
LaVergne TN
LVHW101954220826
846093LV00006B/215

* 9 7 8 9 3 5 4 6 2 2 5 4 0 *